A STUDY OF RELIGIOUS THOUGHT AT OXFORD AND CAMBRIDGE

1590-1640

Stewart A. Dippel

UNIVERSITY
PRESS OF
AMERICA

Lanham • New York • London

Copyright © 1987 by

University Press of America,® Inc.

4720 Boston Way
Lanham, MD 20706

3 Henrietta Street
London WC2E 8LU England

All rights reserved

Printed in the United States of America

British Cataloging in Publication Information Available

Library of Congress Cataloging-in-Publication Data

Dippel, Stewart A., 1950-
  A study of religious thought at Oxford and Cambridge.

  Bibliography: p.
  Includes index.
  1. Theology, Doctrinal—England—History—16th century. 2. Theology, Doctrinal—England—History—17th century. 3. University of Oxford—History—16th century. 4. University of Cambridge—History—16th century. 5. University of Oxford—History—17th century. 6. University of Cambridge—History—17th century. 7. Church of England—Doctrines—History—16th century. 8. Church of England—Doctrines—History—17th century. 9. Puritans—Doctrines—History—16th century. 10. Puritans—Doctrines—History—17th century. 11. Anglican Communion—England—Doctrines—History—16th century. 12. Anglican Communion—England—Doctrines—History—17th century. I. Title.
BT30.G7D57   1987   230'.0942   87-8306
ISBN 0-8191-6387-2 (alk. paper)
ISBN 0-8191-6388-0 (pbk. : alk. paper)

All University Press of America books are produced on acid-free paper which exceeds the minimum standards set by the National Historical Publication and Records Commission.

FOR OUR PARENTS: ARTHUR AND PATRICIA; MIKE AND SHIRLEY

ACKNOWLEDGMENTS

My wife, Martha, and I began our marriage about the same time I began writing this book. I owe her. She kept faith with me all those years. All those years that kept me up until the early morning she kept faith with me.

I also thank the History Department at The Ohio State University for allowing me to participate in their graduate degree program. I thank the College of the Humanities for awarding me a scholarship with which I pursued my studies in England. Consequently, I thank the staff at the British Library, the University Library at Cambridge, and the Bodleian Library at Oxford for their assistance.

I want to thank Ms. Nancy Davis, Ms. Denise Henning and the administrative staff at Daemen College for their assistance in preparing the manuscript for publication. Also, I thank Daemen College for the opportunity to teach there.

More especially, I would like to thank Professors Brad Chapin, James Kittelson, and Clayton Roberts--three men who disagree on everything except integrity--who taught me whatever I know of scholarship.

The greatest debts are always those that cannot be repaid. My father, Arthur, fell to cancer before I could complete this work. Before he died, he made me promise I would finish. In his life, and in his death, he endeavored to teach me something of perseverance--that old Christian virtue. I claim little for the following pages except for their testimonial to perseverance.

TABLE OF CONTENTS

INTRODUCTION ix

- I. THE LIMITS OF LEARNING: THE UNIVERSITY
  EPISTEMOLOGY 1

- II. HEARERS AND DOERS OF THE WORD;
  THE UNIVERSITY THEOLOGY OF FAITH
  AND WORKS 12

- III. THE CALVINIST CONCEPT OF THE TRUE
  CHURCH: ITS IMPACT ON THE UNIVERSITY
  ECCLESIOLOGY 49

- IV. UNIVERSITY THEOLOGY WITHIN A POLITICAL
  CONTEXT 77

- V. PURITANISM, REVOLUTION, AND THE
  UNIVERSITIES 97

BIBLIOGRAPHY 109

INDEX 121

INTRODUCTION

The following chapters investigate theological thought within the universities of Oxford and Cambridge during the half century preceding the English Revolution of 1640. Previous treatments of university history have concentrated primarily upon the institutional and political facets. Such seminal studies by nineteenth century scholars as Rashdall's *The Universities Of Europe In The Middle Ages* (1895), Mallet's *History Of The University Of Oxford* (1924), and Mullinger's *A History Of The University Of Cambridge* (1888) fall within this category. More recent sholarship tends to reflect these earlier proclivities. William T. Costello, for example, studies the institutional framework at Cambridge from the perspective of scholasticism in his *The Scholastic Curriculum At Early Seventeenth Century Cambridge* (1958). Lawrence Stone addresses himself, in such works as *The University In Society* (1974), to an examination of the relationship between universities and social strata.

Surprisingly little scholarly literature exists concerning the English universities during the early modern period. Probably the most prominent scholars who have studied this period are Mark H. Curtis and H.C. Porter. Their respective works, *Oxford And Cambridge In Transition: 1558-1642* (1959) and *Reformation And Reaction In Tudor Cambridge* (1958), constitute the most comprehensive treatment of the subject. Although at times they discuss theological issues, such discussion essentially develops within the more general context of their investigations into the relationship between the university and society. They especially concentrate on political developments, considered from both the secular and religious perspective, within the university. Neither professors Curtis and Porter nor any other scholar have attempted a comprehensive investigation of the early modern English univrsity from a primarily theological orientation. Some scholars, however, have studied university theology within a more narrow framework, narrower both in terms of chronology and topic. Richard Bauckham, for example, in an article which appeared in the *Journal of Ecclesiastical History* (1975), entitled "Marian Exiles and Cambridge Puritanism: James Pilkington's 'Halfe a Score,'" analyzes the transitional tensions of Puritan exiles upon their return to St. John's

College following Elizabeth's accession. Several limitations apply to this and similar investigations. The relatively short span of time covered by these studies limit their usefulness. Secondly, they concentrate on the political manifestations of theology. Finally, they approach university theology with a predetermined categorization of Puritan and Anglican 'schools' of religious thought within the university structure.

This study will concentrate on those aspects of university history largely ignored by scholars. It revises the structural framework with which students have previously chartered their courses into university history. It does not focus on institutional and political history, with an occasional foray into university theology. Instead, it focuses on theology itself, with some attention paid to the intrusion of theology into the institutonal and political spheres. It reverses, in other words, the primary emphasis from the secular to the religious history of Oxford and Cambridge.

This study employs a broader chronological scope than that used by scholars, such as Richard Bauckham, who concentrated on one university during one reign. This study surveys the sixty years leading to the English Revolution of 1640. The most important consideration governing this choice is the uniquely unsettled character of English society during the late Tudor and early Stuart periods. Many historians, notably Christopher Hill in his Intellectual Origins Of The English Revolution (1965) and Carl Bridenbaugh in his Vexed And Troubled Englishmen: 1590-1642 (1968), have noted and emphasized the unusual degree of ferment and dislocation which beset England during those years. The question immedately presents itself: to what extent did this intellectual restlessness infect university theologians? Does the development of university theology, in other words, reflect the same ferment which characterized society as a whole during the period? This investigation does not extend beyond 1640 for two reasons. During the twenty years of revolutionary turmoil university history merged with the general political and religious history of the nation and, as such, ceased to have any independent existence. Secondly, the theology which emerged at the universites and characterized the post-Restoration theologians, being preponderantly rationalistic, differed radically from its earlier counterpart. Historians such as William Cecil de Pauley in his The Candle Of The Lord: Studies In The Cambridge Platonists (1937) have thoroughly recounted this transformation. Therefore, from the perspective of both the content of university theology and the academic literature regarding that theology, an investigation beyond the Restoration logically falls beyond the scope of this study.

In contrast to the studies noted above, the thematic thrust of the following pages does not follow the traditional pattern of an Anglican/Puritan dichotomy. This inquiry does not postulate a priori conclusions to the effect that an Anglican/Puritan controversy existed with reference to every theological issue within the university community. To be sure, some issues provoked differences which materialized in Anglican and Puritan polarities. Such situations have been noted. Likewise, with regards to those questions which failed to elicit distinctively Anglican and Puritan perspectives, the study assumes a consensus of opinion. With respect to a related concern, this study does not accept the standard distinction between 'Puritan' Cambridge and 'Anglican' Oxford. Such scholars as Professor Curtis have questioned this stereotype. Cambridge included its share of 'Anglicans' and, similarly, Oxford its share of 'Puritans.' Moreover, such an assumption violates the supposition inherent in this study, namely, that Anglican and Puritan 'schools' within the university should not be presumed.

Manuscript collections housed in the British Library, the University Library at Cambridge and the Bodleian Library at Oxford constitute the sources for this inquiry. These manuscripts include several types; namely, sermons and lectures written completely out by professors, student notes on those sermons and lectures, disputations, university court proceedings, and correspondence among university administrators and professors as well as between university and Crown personnel. With the exception of sermon and lecture material, almost all data relative to persons and places are known and cited. Unfortunately, much of the lecture and sermon material is either anonymous or dateless. In such cases the citation may only be identified by the college and/or university from which it came. Approximate dates suggest themselves occssionally on the basis of internal evidence.

Aside from manuscript sources the study incorporates pertinent primary sources published during the period. Also, an occasional reference is made to the secondary literature on the subject where that literature directly and importantly addresses some of the questions posed by this study. This study, however, is not an historiographical essay; rather, it is an attempt to develop a series of arguments whose proofs are drawn from unpublished sources and to avoid as much as possible merely entering into dialogue on the issues and controversies which grace the secondary literature. Finally, with regard to the study's methodology, it makes little effort to trace the chronological progression of those aspects of university thought that remained essentially unchanged throughout the period. Only those issues which produced significant developments over a given period of time are traced chronologically.

The study begins with an investigation into the relationship between epistemology and theology. The first chapter discusses problems arising from that relationship and the solutions offered by university theologians. One problem which presented itself to university theologians concerned the extent to which epistemological and theological objectives coincided. Another problem, or rather doubt, involved the question relative to the extent to which epistemology could satisfactorily address itself to theological issues. This chapter seeks to show how the university theologians solved both these problems.

The second chapter investigates the most important theological question addressed at the universities. That is the soteriological problem. It was the most important issue because it tended to provide the centripetal force holding the discussion of other theological issues to a central point. University soteriology followed in part from the epistemological framework. University theologians postulated a close relationship between religious knowledge and salvation. The most pressing soteriological question, of course, involved the proper relationship between faith and works in the salvation process. This question, in turn, presupposed an answer to the controversy over the relative efficacy of free will. It is the purpose of chapter two to show how the university theologians answered these and related questions.

The third chapter raises the highly controversial issue of ecclesiology. In both universities the Puritans made an unsuccessful attempt to impose the Calvinist ecclesiology upon the Elizabethan settlement. The purpose of chapter three is to define the Calvinist ecclesiology, to show how far it permeated the university, and to show why it ultimately failed to win acceptance.

The fourth chapter begins with an investigation of the institutional influence exerted upon university theologian by both the university administration and the Crown. What was the scope and success of the Crown's attempt to impose its view of religious conformity? What resistance did university administrators and theologians make to the Crown's endeavors? Did university administrators and professors differ in terms of their perceptions of and reactions to Crown policy? What were the political ramifications of university theology?

Chapter five investigates the relationship between the political ramifications of university theology and the English Revolution of 1640. Did the university theologians knowingly or unknowingly prepare the way for the English Revolution? May we speak in terms of a conservative political ideology extrapolated from Anglicanism with reference to Oxford and Cambridge? How deeply did Puritanism, defined in terms of a revolutionary ideology, permeate the universities?

CHAPTER I

THE LIMITS OF LEARNING; THE UNIVERSITY EPISTEMOLOGY

This chapter attempts to answer the following questions. How did the universities define the purpose of education? More specifically, did university theologians identify with the Medieval or Renaissance educational objectives? Secondly, what limits did university theologians place upon their overall epistemological horizon? Did they reference their epistemology, in other words, within an optimistic or pessimistic framework? Thirdly, to what extent did skepticism relative to the attainment of an absolute religious knowledge engender consequences for university theology? Finally, what basis, if any, existed for the foundation of a comprehensive and an optimistic attitude towards theological knowledge?

Roger Ascham, Fellow of St. John's College at Cambridge and tutor for Elizabeth I, lamented the contemporary status of English education in The Scholemaster (1570). Few students during the sixteenth-century ever "come to show any great countenance, or bear any great authority abroad in the world, but either live obscurely, men know not how, or die obscurely, men mark not when."[1] In many ways Ascham irradiated the essence of Elizabethan humanism. His career and his treatise reflected a belief that education should direct itself to the aspirations and concerns of man within a secular context. His earlier work, Toxophilus (1545), after all, advocated a correlation between physical exercise (i.e., archery) and emotive or intellectual growth. As such, it epitomized the concerns of man secularly construed. The complaint noted above indirectly described the ideal enunciated by secular humanism throughout the Renaissance. Education should provide the necessary requisites for success and recognition in both the public and private spheres.

Ascham wrote The Scholemaster within the framework of the court. As such, that treatise more faithfully reflected the intellectual atmosphere pervading the court than that surrounding the universities and characteristic of England in general. The atmosphere at court, during Elizabeth's reign, exuded the secularism of Italian humanism during the Renaissance. The universities advocated a somewhat different ideal. Still, to some degree, medieval in their perception of education's purpose, they

1

contended that knowledge of theology and its practical applications constituted the proper educational ideal. An Oxford faculty member expressed this older attitude during a lecture on St. Paul's epistle to Titus delivered, probably, in 1600. That apostle, he said:

> doth teach you what you should cheefely desire to heere & learne of us; not how to bee able to dispute & contend about matters of historie or genealogie; not how to moove vaine & foolish questions, not how to bee deep sighted in misteries of more curiositie than goodness or profitt; but rather how to know god aright & his sonne Jesus Christ & him crucified; how to feare & serve him in spirit & trugh wthout hypocrisise; how to beeleeve rightly in god & manifest our faith in rightuousnes, how to mortifie the old man wth the affections & lusts thereof; how to build up the new man in holines, & work out your salvation wth feare & tremblinge; all wch are good & profitable unto men.[2]

Students should not immerse themselves in such unprofitable disciplines as history. Rather, they should study the right knowledge of God and its application towards a religious life. In somewhat the same manner, a Cambridge theologian noted the distinction between true and false knowledge. "Believe ye wysdome of God," he warned, "not ye entisynge & deceitfull speeches either of philosophers that are counted learned, or of Orators yt are esteemed to be Eloquente, or of Doctors that set foorthe Fables."[3] Education should impart some measure of divine wisdom. Anything which strayed from this primary objective not only strayed from the proper purpose of education, but from the truth as well.

A paradox existed with reference to this educational ideal. On the one hand, university professors emphasized the necessity of construing education within a theological context. On the other hand, they doubted whether the institutional university could accomplish that objective. The apostles, after all, held no university degrees. Roger Some, Master of Peterhouse College at Cambridge and Vice Chancellor to that university, expressed such a reluctance. "Our Savior Christ did not send any universitie men at the first to preach the Gospel," he observed, "least the conversion of men should be attributed to learning and eloquence. He called rude and base men from their occupations to be his Apostles."[4] Not formally educated men but the unlearned had first effected the apostolic function. Roger Some did not share Renaissance humanism's great regard, in an exclusive sense, for academic expertise relative to religious issues. Mere "learning and eloquence," divorced from a theological orientation, might render the universities too secularly predisposed to attain their proper ideal.

Even if the universities avoided such a secular orientation, their theologians tended to doubt the efficacy of attaining a complete and total knowledge of God. While their educational goal demonstrated a medieval orientation, their expectations relative to that objective reflected the skeptical epistemology characteristic of Renaissance humanism. Ever since Petrarca denigrated scholastic pretentions to comprehensive learning in De sui ipsius et multorum ignorantia, the elusive probability of any absolute knowledge sporadically presented itself to scholars.[5] As late as 1625 Master Lushington, an Oxford theologian, addressed the problem of certain knowledge in the curse of a sermon delivered upon the resurrection. As a general principle he readily asserted the futility of absolute knowledge.

> Nay to follow ye old philosophers, & say there is noe truth at all, noe certaine knowledge is not so absurd as some pretend it. We have noe true knowledge, true knowledge is to know things as they are, to comprehend yr nature, & to know ym: as much as tis possible they can be knowen, & soe a man scarce knowes a strawe. True knowledge is reserved for another life, where we shal know things as they are & know as we are knowen. Here we may have some qualified notions & modified apprehentions, but comprehend nothing; we know nothing as we ought, soe yn we may have some knowledge of ye truth. But noe true knowledge, especialy of yt we should know.[6]

Man's epistemic impotence, he continued, increases relative to the importance of the truth he trys to ascertain. Our knowledge of God and of the means to a religious life, the especial knowledge that we should assimilate, remains inherently less certain than our knowledge of more mundane subjects.

In the same sermon, Master Lushington suggested several possibilities in explanation of this impotence.

> The reason is things are not here represented as they are. Their verity & essence enters not into us, for if soe al thinges should be knowne of all alike & after ye same fastion. Truth being uniforme in it selfe should be of like creditt & qualitie through out ye whole world. But things are apprehended according to ye proportion & capacity of our conceipts, yeelding & submitting themselves to ye humor & complection of our understanding, wch: is as various as our severall temperments. Wt another conceives I cannot, though uppon ye same evidence. & there is noe great hold to wt I my selfe conceived for wt I believed yesterday I may doubt of today & to morrow find my selfe quite deceived.

A platonic dualism pervades the world and thus its epistemology. Truth's "verity & essence" presumably exists in an Ideal heaven divorced from man's environment and indeed from his very being. Left to himself man formulates erratic truths which vary among men and even within each man changes as the seasons. Outside of the Platonic world of Ideas, truth remains subjective. Some men of greater "capacity" and "understanding" may more closely perceive truth, but even their 'truths' remain partial an uncertain.

The concern of some university theologians relative to such a limited knowledge prompted pressing questions pertinent to the status of fallen man. The divorce between an absolute truth and man's relative and imperfect truth necessarily implied a more catastrophic divorce between God and man. Ignorance invariably spawned sin. Aided only by an imperfect and inadequate knowledge of God, man's resultant inability to apply an absolute theology towards a religious life irrevocably must result in evil. Man could not obey God if he failed to understand God's nature and God's will for man. Preaching in the mid-1630s upon the correspoding distincitions which St. Paul drew in Ephesians 5:8 between light/grace and darkness/condemnation, and Oxford faculty member drew his own analogy between darkness and ignorance which resulted in sin. "The state of sin is a state of blindness," he argued, and "every sinner is a perfect ignoramus."[8] Another Oxford theologian who discussed Genesis during the same period asserted the same cause and effect relationship between limited knowledge and evil. "There bee 2 evils from whence all others doe proceed," he observed, "ignorance in ye understanding, & concupiscence in ye will."[9] Imperfect knowledge deteriorated man's will, and evil resulted. The concern over the limit and extent of man's knowledge was not merely an academic concern. It touched upon the great questions centering around man's salvation. Could an epistemology of hope replace one of despair?

More than any other factor, the educational possibilities inherent in a learned ministry provided the foundation for a more optimistic epistemology. Through a unique integration of ministerial and scholarly attributes the universities essayed a more comprehensive knowledge of God. In much the same manner, although within a primarily secular context, Italian humanists earlier conceptualized a union of rhetoric and philosophy.[10] English universites simply substituted the function of minster for orator. Indeed, the universities asserted the total inadequacy of ministers devoid of scholarly qualities or of scholars who lacked godly characteristics. "They must go together," wrote Roger Some, for

> learning without godlinesses is as a gold ring upon a swine's snoute. Godlinesse in a minister, without learning, is as a faire colour without light to shew it by, and as a goodly bell without a clapper.[11]

Minister-scholars, however, through a synthesis of their distinctive traits might achieve a more absolute theology.

In his treatise __Of The Calling Of The Ministerie__ William Perkins, Fellow of Christ's College at Cambridge during the closing decades of the sixteenth century, declared scholarship to be an indispensable element of the ministry. Since "every true Minister must be God's __interpreter__ to the people, and the people's to God," he wrote, "then hence we learne, that every one, who either is, or intends to be a minister, must have that _toong of the learned._" In his definition of the ministerial role, seen from the perspective of divine inspiration, Perkins isolated the peculiar asset rendering that role conducive to a more enhanced knowledge of God. God directly imparted learning to his minister-scholars. Ministers "must be inwardly learned" according to Perkins and "taught by the spirit of God." Through a special revelation "a true Minister must bee inwardly taught by the spiritual school-maister the holy Ghost."[12] Such divine intervention in the educational process expanded the epistemological horizon.

The great danger in advocating an epistemological role for divine inspiration involved placing too great an emphasis upon inspiration and special revelation at the expense of the study of scripture. The proper relationship betweeen an inspirational epistemology and an epistemology rooted in traditional scriptural exegesis plagued Reformation thought from its inception. Both Luther and Calvin wrestled with the problem and both men warned against permitting inspiration to play an autonomous role. Calvin, for example, strongly emphasized the inspirational functon played by the Holy Spirit. However, he stressed just as strongly that the Holy Spirit expressed itself through and accommodated itself to the Word. An inspirational epistemology, in other words, must fully integrate itself with traditional scriptural exegesis.[13] Perkins asserted precisely the same position. "Let no man thinke I heere give the least allowance to Anabaptisticall fancies and revelations," he warned,

> for they contemne both humane learning, and the studie of the scripture, and trust wholy to revelations of the spirit; but God's spirit worketh not but upon the foundation of the word.[14]

Inspirational epistemology must avoid the theological chaos of "Anabaptisticall fancies" by tying itself to traditional scholarship.

In the course of his polemics with the Radical Reformers Luther identified the same erroneous tendency consequent to an unfettered inspirational theory. For him such license signified false prophecy.[15] In 1637 a Fellow of Balliol College at Oxford found in the text Ezekiel 3:17 ample opportunity to discuss the "office & duty" of the prophet. Sensing the dangers inherent in an office

devoid of traditional restraints, the theologian
defined the prohpet's twofold duty:

> 1ly. Respecting god to heare ye word;
> 2ly. Respecting ye people to give ym warning.[16]

Prophetic "warning" must correlate with the injunction
"to heare ye word." Legitimate inspiration must
express itself through scriptural exegesis. Another
Oxford Fellow emphasized the same point in a discourse
upon I Kings 13:26 delivered the same year. "Hee was
a prophet & therefore wee have a faire ground to
assure ourselves of the trueth of this story,"
admitted the theologian,

> butt wee have a stronger ground for our
> faith then that; viz. in yt wee have it
> recorded in God's booke. This wee must
> make ye cheife, nay ye onely ground of
> our faith; not humane revelation, tho of
> a prophet, tho of a Paul, or an Angell
> from heaven.[17]

Clearly the inspirational function, while legitimate,
must not supersede the academic function.

Despite the above qualifications, divine
inspiration provided the most important encouragement
for a more ambitious epistemology. Minister-scholars,
rather than mere ministers or mere scholars, offered
the best hope for an absolute knowledge of God and of
the means towards godly living. The emphasis of the
humanists on man's dignity, derived primarily from the
Genesis account of creation, offered another basis for
optimism relative to a more comprehensive
epistemology.[18]

In 1625 an Oxford theologian discussed Matthew
3:2. That text addressed the subject of repentance.
However, the theologian chose not man's depravity, but
rather man's dignity, as his initial point of
departure. "Neither was man barely made a lumpish &
unfashioned heape of rude materials," he asserted with
reference to the appropriate Genesis texts,

> but he was formed of ye dust of ye earth
> & yt in ye most exuisite & rarest shape
> of all creatures. For in ye image &
> likenes of his creator was he made in
> righteousness & perfect holines.[19]

Man, of course, fell from this exalted state. Nevertheless, a spark of his former excellence, the synteresis, remained and prevented him from a totally catastrophic descent to the level of bestial ignorance. That remnant of dignity constituted the basis for a greater knowledge of God's will and thus it provided the basis for repentance. It provided the means to a more absolute theology. "Is any man so brutish as to loose his understanding faculty in ye perception of this meanes?" this theologian rhetorically asked.[20]

Dr. Silby, another Oxford Fellow, taught his class the proper interpretation of James 1:14, which text dealt with temptation. He, also, alluded to man's dignity in his exegesis. Dr. Silby mirrored Pico della Mirandola's classic enunciation of that theme in the _Oration On The Dignity Of Man_. Man's nature, according to Dr. Silby, admitted of either an upward ascent towards a fuller understanding of God and of his desires relative to man or, lamentably, a descent into ignorance and sin. "Man has a middle nature between good and bad angels," Dr. Silby told his class, and "as his nature is so is he good or bad: a vesell of honour or dishonour."[21] Man's intrinsic dignity implied latent capabilities pertinent to our understanding of God and his will toward us which, in turn provided the means to identify and resist temptation.

If God made man in his image and likeness, then the universities need not postulate a limited epistemology. Man's nature enabled him to construct a more comprehensive theology. Moreover, God did not abandon man in his search for knowledge. Through inspirational insights imparted to his minister-scholars through the Holy Spirit, God facilitated the educational process. Despite well-grounded doubts, the universities formulated an epistemology of hope. Nor did the universities approach epistemology from a merely academic perspective. Their epistemological focus always centered on the theological means by which man attained saving grace. In a preface entitled "To All Ignorant People That Desire To Be Instructed," William Perkins emphasized the relationship between ignorance/damnation and knowledge/salvation. "Now where ignorance raigneth there raignes sinne," he admonished, "and where sinne raignes there the devill rules. And where he rules men are in a damnable case."[22]

[10] The assimilation of rhetoric and philosophy is the principal theme developed by Jerrold E. Seigel, _Rhetoric And Philosophy In Renaissance Humanism: The Union Of Eloquence And Wisdom, Petrarch To Valla_ (Princeton: Princeton University Press, 1968). Renaissance humanists placed more emphasis on philosophy/wisdom than on rhetoric/eloquence. However, they construed philosophy/wisdom within a secular context. It meant a knowledge of virtue and the application of such knowledge towards a virtuous life. Appropriately, Professor Seigel has emphasized Petrarca in that regard. See e.g. pp. 36ff. Their epistemology, in other words, was not theologically oriented.

[11] Some, _A Godly Treatise_, p. 185.

[12] William Perkins, _Of The Calling Of The Ministerie. Two Treatises. Describing The Duties and Dignities of that calling. Delivered Publikely in the Universitie of Cambridge by Maister Perkins_ (London: Thomas Creede, 1606), pp. 3 and 4.

[13] Scholars have thoroughly investigated the role played by divine inspiration in Calvin's theology. See, e.g., H. Jackson Forstman, _Word And Spirit: Calvin's Doctrine Of Biblical Authority_ (Stanford: Stanford University Press, 1962). See pp. 14 and 64 for Calvin's acknowledgement of the inspirational role relative to our understanding and knowledge of God. For Calvin's identification of that role within the context of the Word, see p. 49. One should not, however, adopt the view that Calvin, or for that matter Luther, placed rationality/scholarship above inspiration. For an excellent treatment of Calvin's epistemology construed within the contemporary evidentialist debate, see Kenneth Konyndyk's "Faith and Evidentialism" in Robert Audi and William J. Wainwright, eds., _Rationality, Religious Belief, & Moral Commitment: New Essays in the Philosophy of Religion_ (Ithaca, New York: Cornell University Press, 1986), pp. 82-108. Basically, Professor Konyndyk argues that Calvin's emphasis upon illumination/inspiration through the Holy Spirit does not allow him to travel to far down the evidentialist road.

[14] Perkins, _Of The Calling Of The Ministerie_, p. 4.

NOTES

[1] Roger Ascham, *The Scholemaster* (1570). Cited by Roy Lamson and Hallett Smith, eds., *The Golden Hind: An Anthology of Elizabethan Prose And Poetry* (NY: W.W. Norton & Company, Inc., 1942), p. 89.

[2] London, British Library, Sloane MSS, 227, "Theological lectures and sermons delivered by a member of St. Mary Hall before the University of Oxford about the year 1600," p. 48.

[3] Cambridge, University Library, MS.Gg.1.29, "A Collection of Miscellaneous Theological and Historical Documents," fol. 3b.

[4] Roger Some, *A Godly Treatise containing and deciding certaine questions, mooved of late in London and other places, touching the Ministerie, Sacraments and Church* (London: Christopher Barker, 1588), p. 57.

[5] Recent scholarship has established fairly well the skeptical nature which characterized much of Renaissance humanism. Such skepticism distinguished humanistic epistemology from that of both the Medieval and Reformation eras. Professor James Kittelson has illustrated the importance of these differences in epistemology with his argument that the transition from a cautious to a certain epistemology constituted a central motif in the transformation of humanist types into reforming types. See James M. Kittelson, *Wolfgang Capito: From Humanist To Reformer* (Leiden: brill, 1975), pp. 50, 81, 140, 169, and 207.

[6] Oxford, Bodleian Library, MS.ADD.B.82, "Mr. Lushington's sermon preached at St. Maries Oxon: April 18, 1625," p. 13.

[7] Ibid.

[8] Oxford, Bodleian Library, MS.Eng.th.f.17, "Sermon Noates (1634-1637), taken from the Preaching of Hoffman, Sutton, Chidloo, Pell, Digle, Stanly, Archer, Fisher and other eminent Oxford Preachers," p. 24.

[9] Ibid., p. 54.

[15] For Luther's identification and definition of false prophets, see Mark Edwards, Jr., *Luther And The False Brethren* (Stanford: Stanford Univrsity Press, 1975).

[16] Oxford, Bodleian Library, MS.Eng.th.f.7, p. 149.

[17] Ibid., p. 126.

[18] An extensive study of humanist conceptualizations of man's nature in general, and the Italian Renaissance's attitude towards man's dignity in specific, may be found in Charles Trinkaus, *In Our Image And Likeness: Humanity and Divinity in Italian Humanist Thought,* 2 vols. (London: Constable & Co., Ltd., 1970). The humanistic exaltation of man's dignity, noted Trinkaus, "is possibly the most affirmative view of human nature in the history of thought and expression." p. xiv.

[19] Oxford, Bodleian Library, MS.ADD.B.82, p. 17.

[20] Ibid., p. 19.

[21] Oxford, Bodleian Library, MS.ADD.A.115, "Autograph Manuscript A.D. 1595: The Common-Place Book of the Rev. Lionel Day, Fellow of Balliol College, Oxford," p. 86.

[22] William Perkins, *The Foundation Of Christian Religion gathered into sixe Principles* (Cambridge: John Legat, 1603), preface.

Chapter II

HEARERS AND DOERS OF THE WORD:
THE UNIVERSITY THEOLOGY OF FAITH AND WORKS

"Let us assure our selves that at the day of Doom men shall be judged according to their fruits," Christian told Faithful during the course of their pilgramage. "It will not be said then _Did you believe?_ " admonished Christian, "but Were you _Doers,_ or _Talkers_ only? and accordingly shall they be judged."[1] So wrote John Bunyan in Pilgrim's Progress (1678). In this passage, indeed throughout the entire allegory, Bunyan asserted the superiority of works over faith relative to man's salvation. _Pilgrim's Progress,_ after all, displayed a striking resemblance to medieval morality plays. "I never went to school to Aristotle or Plato," Bunyan once reflected. Although Bunyan never received a formal education he nevertheless fell heir to a climate of opinion created by the universities within which the soteriological dialogue took place. Years earlier, at the turn of the seventeenth century, an unknown Oxford theologian anticipated almost verbatim Bunyan's argument. "I would exhort all men unto the diligent hearinge & readinge of god's word; especiallie unto the doeinge & keepinge of the same," he instructed his students, "because not the hearers, not the readers, but the doers shalbee justified."[2] Faith, in other words, possesses no efficacy apart from works.

Aside, perhaps, from ecclesiological questions, the questions relative to the nature of the salvation process constituted the most important and controversial theological issue during the sixteenth and seventeenth centuries.[3] The universities characteristically structured their theology around a framework founded on the answers to such questions. Even religious issues not directly related to soteriology, such as the dialogue pertinent to original sin and the dignity of man, invariably centered on the question of salvation. Many university Fellows, such as the Oxford theologian noted above, explicity elucidated their theology within the soteriological context. Others formulated their theology through implicit references to it. In either case, most theological thought within the universities radiated from such a soteriological core.

Pursuant to this centrality, this chapter attempts

to answer two basic questions. The first such
question relates, in general, to the nature of the
relationship between soteriology and epistemology.
Did the university epistemology suggest a framework
within which the university soteriology operated? Did
it, in other words, define the terms of the
discussion? Another question relative to this
relationship asks whether epistemology, construed in
terms of content pertinent to the knowledge of God,
contributed to the direction of soteriological
thought? The second broad question involves the
relationship between faith and works in the salvation
process. This question, of course, subsumes many
others. What did university theologians mean by the
terms faith and works? What were the implications of
their meanings for such related polarities as
law/gospel and reason/revelation? How did they
perceive the role played by the Word in the salvation
process? Finally, and perhaps most importantly, how
did the debate relative to predestination and free
will affect their soteriology?

The theology of salvation discussed below is, I
believe, fairly representative of university opinion
on the subject. If I may anticipate somewhat the
ensuing argument, the soteriology outlined below is a
moderate soterilogy. That is to say, it is neither
exclusively Puritan nor exclusively Anglican in its
orientation. Of course one may interpret the term
'moderate' to mean 'moderately Puritan' or 'moderately
Anglican.' I suspect one's proclivity here is
predicated largely upon subjective prejudice. In any
event, my point is that the term 'moderate'
presupposes an interfusion of both Anglican and
Puritan elements. It is not necessary to presume an
either Anglican or Puritan soteriology. With respect
to an Anglican/Puritan terminology regarding the
salvation issue, I concur with Professor Peter Lake in
his "attempt to transcend the crude dichotomy between
conflict and consensus which seems to beset the recent
historiography of the early modern period."[4] This is
not to deny that some university theologians advocated
an exclusively Anglican or Puritan theology in general
and soteriology in particular. Some of them did. In
so far as soteriological issues are concerned,
however, neither the printed nor the manuscript
sources indicate that such extreme viewpoints
constituted a prevailing and characteristic university
opinion on the sotriological issue. Rather it is the
moderate sotriology, the view of salvation discussed
below, which most accurately depicts a representative

13

university consensus relative to this issue.

The universities approached the issue of salvation from a secure epistemological perspective. Epistemology and soteriology seemed to mutually reinforce each other. "The first thinge to bee learned in religion," observed an unknown Oxford Fellow, "is a right knowledge of those things wch wee ought to know & beeleeve to our soules health concerning god."[5] Soteriology, presumably the issue of the soul's health referred to the salvation process, constituted a fundamental epistemological objective. Lecturing his students in 1590 on the nature of faith, Laurence Chaderton, Master of Emmanuel College at Cambridge, observed that man will never attain to a "perfect faith because he can never have perfect knowledge." One of the characteristics of what Chaderton identified as "a weak faith" is that it is a faith "where knowedge faileth."[6] Thus, for Chaderton imperfect knowledge impaired the salvation process. For university theologians the proper religious and educational objectives tended to coincide. "True religion," noted the Oxford Fellow cited above, consisted of a "a right knowledge of god & a right worship of god."[7] Epistemology correctly conceived naturally identified and resulted in the correct soteriology. The purposes of soteriology and epistemology, in short, were identical.

The universities adamantly insisted, moreover, that these synonymous objectives should be addressed primarily, if not exclusively, within their broad institutional framework. These "high points of religion" and "deepe misteries of divinitie," explained the Oxford theologian noted above, should be excluded from the discussion of "men of base condition." Such men:

> will ordinarilie reason & dispute of them, in alehouses, & tavernes amidest their full cuppes, & in their drunken panges will not spare to sett their mouthes against heaven & to blaspheme god himself.[8]

The Fellow expressed his desire that the authorities silence such men and insure:

> that it might bee lawfull only for the godlie, wise & learned to reason of divine misteries, & that only in places

> convenient, upon mature deliberation wth great reverence. Then would not religion want her due estimation, as now it doth; nor learninge bee out of date as now it is.[9]

"Places convenient" presumably referred to the university setting and "mature deliberation wth great reverence" probably meant a highly structured or formalized atmosphere such as a lecture or disputation. Only men of learning, that is to say, the minister-scholars and their students identified in the previous chapter, possessed the attributes necessary to engender a purposeful discussion on the subject of salvation. The universities, in brief, confidently believed that from the perspective of both content (curricula) and personnel, questions of salvation[10] naturally and legitimately fell within their province.

The first prerequisite relative to the issue of salvation, then, consisted of a more comprehensive knowledge of God. Such knowledge provided the foundation upon which to build the soteriological ediface. Regardless of whether theologians addressed questions of salvation from the perspective of faith or from that of works, they prefaced their inquiries with assertions of the necessity of such a foundation. "The knowledge of god beegetteth in us faith & love," argued another unknown Oxford Fellow, and

> the more wee grow in grace, & in the knowledge of god, the more wee beeleeve in god & the more entirely wee love god. The more wee beeleeve in god & love god the more care of doinge his will & keepinge his commandements; such a connextion there is of knowledge, faith, & love towards god, that where all are not there is neither.[11]

Of special interest here is the causal relationship between knowledge/faith/love. Both faith and works (love) followed from an enhanced knowledge of God. Indeed, such knowledge constituted the cornerstone of the salvation process.

Some such enhanced knowledge resulted in part from the application of the principles of negative theology. Especially popular with humanists, this concept asserted that theologians ascertain God's nature by first ascertaining those attributes not characteristic of God. Negative theology stressed the use of reason in the discernment of the natural order. Through use of the critical faculty theologians delineated non-natural, and thus non-Godly, elements. An Oxford theologian applied this concept while developing the argument that God might be identified without recourse to scriptural authority. "As in my former lecture by the discourse of naturall reason I proved a deitie," the Fellow observed, "soe now likewise because they approve not the veritie of the Scriptures, I will in few words by the same discourse of reason tell them what god is--at least wise what god is not."[12] Thus, atheists have no excuse for their ignorance of God. Secure in this premise the theologian "inferred" that God possessed in greater degree all the attributes and blessing which He bestowed upon His creation. Accordingly, "God hath a more excellent being & a more spirituall understandinge" than anything in His world. "Wherefore I conclude," the theologian observed,

> that the contraries unto these; namelie not to bee, not to live, not to feele, not to understand, are opposite unto god. That all not beeinge--that death, that insensibilitie, that ignorance, that all imperfections are infinitely removed from him.[13]

Infinity in being, in other words, constituted a principal divine attribute which followed necessarily from the obvious truth that God could not be less finite than His creation. Of special interest here, with reference to our previous discussion of epistemology, the professor observed that "ignorance" is a concept contrary to God's nature. From the perspective of salvation, as well, the concept of "death" constitutes an idea alien to God. From God's infinite being the theologian proceeded to enumerate other divine characteristics. "It doth most necessarilie follow that hee is the most perfect & actuall & absolute beeing," continued the theologian:

> god is an interminent beeinge, infinite, eternall, wthout beeginninge wthout ende; that god is in everie place, for otherwise hee should have non esse loci--a not beeing of place-- wch is infinitely repugnant to his infinit beeinge. Wherfore if they will beeleeve

> reason they must wth us acknowledge god to bee of infinite vertue, power, wisedome, maiestie, to whom only the power of creatinge things may bee attributed... That God's understandinge beeinge the same wth his essence is also infinit; as is his beeinge, & that all things in the world have their beeing in god. And knowledge beeinge the same wth his essence, must needs know all thinges in the world, all things visible & invisible, whatsoever hath bin or is now, or shalbee hereafter in the world.[14]

The theologian noted, in short, God's perfection, omnipotence, omnipressence, and omniscience.

Fortunately, the university theologians refused to rely exclusively upon the concept of a negative theology in order to increase their knowledge of God. They incorporated within their thought Luther's distinction between __deus absconditus__ and __deus revelatus.__[15] Much of God's nature, __deus absconditus,__ remained hidden by His choice. To a certain extent, however, God chose to eschew obscurity. God's revelation through scripture provided an added dimension to our understanding. Accordingly, the Oxford theologian noted in the previous paragraph prefaced his lectures with the following remarks within the context of __deus revelatus:__

> For as much as it hath pleased god to reveale his backe parts unto us in the law; & to shew us the light of his Countenance in the gospell, to manifest himselfe unto us in his worde soe farre as necessarie for us to know, & as our humane weaknes is in this life able to comprehend; I will, by the helpe of god's holie spirit, shew you what god is as I myself have learned out of his sacred worde.[16]

The two key points in this statement are: (1) our knowledge of God follows in large part from His revelation of Himself to us in the law and the gospel; and, (2) that revelation is accomplished through the mediating role of the Holy Spirit expressed in the Word.

For most university theologians scriptural

exegesis revolved around the law/gospel axis. The justice/mercy axis represented an allied, almost synonymous dichotomy. The law exemplified God's justice and the gospel His mercy. Only scripture identified these attributes. Other theological methodologies failed to recognize and describe these characteristics. In October of 1636 Master Chidloo lectured on Acts 17:31 at Oxford. The text spoke of judgment ("Because he hath appointed a day in which he will judge the world in righteousness") and, appropriately, the Fellow noted that "these words sett foorth unto us God's two principall attributes: his mercy & Justice"[17] Earlier that year another Oxford Fellow developed an analogous argument during a lecture on I Corinthians 6:9. Again, the text warned of judgment. Accordingly, the theologian admonished his audience not to emphasize God's mercy at the expense of a healthy awareness of His judgment. For they should "know yt hell was made for ye manifestation of God's justice as well as heaven for his mercy."[18] As a final example, Master Stanly, of Magdalen College at Oxford, lectured his students to the same point in February of 1636, while addresing the topic of judgment relative to II Corinthians 5:10. Rest assured "that yr shall bee a generall judgment of all ye world," spoke Master Stanly, in which the "wicked" and the "godly" will finally get their just rewards. At that time the "mistery" of "ye present prosperity of ye wicked" will be solved. Until that final eschatological moment, we must presume on God's judgment based upon the perspective of His revelation to us in terms of this time and place. "God doubtles will make knowne ye equity of his wayes," concluded Master Stanly.[19] Through a final, and complete, revelation at the last judgment, in other words, the distinction between _deus absconditus_ and _deus revelatus_ would be obliterated. Our knowledge of God with respects to His justice/mercy (and, presumably, law/gospel) will then be complete.

The proper relationship between God's mercy and His justice directly touched upon the question of salvation. Accordingly, Master Chidloo addressed the soteriological issue immediately after his observation noted above. "O lett us labour to conforme our wills to god's will," he suggested.

> Is hee willinge to save us & shall wee bee unwillinge to it? Nay wilfully worke out our owne destruction? Hee hath sworne yt hee wills not ye death of him yt dyeth; hee even strives &

> contends to save us. If to become miserable, nay if to dye will do it, hee will undergoe it for us.[20]

Clearly, Master Chidloo emphasized God's mercy and believed that God intended man's salvation. A large part of God's mercy consisted in warning man that punishment and damnation necessarily ensued if he failed to conform himself to God's will. "Now ye trueth of ys his mercy in warninge before hee punish is manifest," said Master Chidloo. For proof:

> aske thy fathers & they will tell thee; search ye Scriptures--those faithfull records of god's proceedinges; see it in our first parents in ye Old World; in Cain; in Sodome & Gomorrah; in Pharaoh & ye Egyptians; in Nimevah; every where particulars of ys kind are infinite. I will appeale to every one's conscience wt good motions hath hee wrought in our harts wch wee have quenched?[21]

Man's conscience serves as a conduit through which God issues his warnings that he holds man accountable before the judgment seat. Conscience constitutes an aid to salvation. As such it demonstrates God's mercy. Mercy, perhaps, exceeded justice in that it always proceeded, and sometimes, followed, judgment. God, in short, always prefaced His judgments with merciful warnings to endangered sinners.

Master Chidloo obviously thought God to be a beneficent entity. Such beneficience applied both to God's mercy and His justice. Some thirty years earlier, another Oxford Fellow lectured his students to the same effect. "Concerning therfore those thinges wch are spoken of god in holie scriptures," he observed, "wee are principallie to regard the unspeakable goodness of god." This goodness consisted, to a considerable extent, of acknowledging our imperfect nature and, as a consequence, dealing gently with us. His goodness manifested itself in the context of _deus revelatus._ God is "a spirituall & invisible substance farre removed from our sences & farre exceeding the weak apprehension of our understandinge" who mercifully "would vouchsafe to applie himselfe to our humane frailtie & infirmitie." God's anthropomorphic appearance, for example, exemplifies this goodness. Each "bodilie part" signifies "unto us certaine of his properties." The ears, for instance, demonstrate "his readines to heere the crie of the afflicted."[22] Indeed, almost any attribute of God might be explained with reference to God's goodness. Even those actions of God which at first glance appear far removed from God's beneficience are, upon closer examination, in truth the actions of a kind and loving God. Master Shirley of Christ Church struck such a chord in 1635. "Wee shall easily discover God's goodnes in it," noted the theologian with reference to Adam's expulsion from the garden. He continued with an explanation of this apparent paradox:

> For he had no sooner excluded him out of one paradise, but straight hee plotts to possess him in another; no sooner had hee disinherited him of an earthly one, but hee contrives a meanes to procure him an heavenly paradise.[23]

Once again, God's judgment incorporated His mercy and His goodness permeated judgment and mercy. That goodness provided an optimistic framework for soteriological discussion. Whether salvation be through faith or through works, and whether one emphasized judgment or mercy, God's beneficience clearly indicated His desire and preference for man's salvation.

Another Christ Church theologian defined the concept of faith in the course of a lecture delivered, interestingly enough, on the subject of obtaining knowledge of God. As mentioned previously, soteriological and epistemological objectives coincided to a considerable extent for university theologians. In associating faith with knowledge, Master Price reiterated standard Reformed thought. Writing on English Calvinism, Professor R. T. Kendall has observed that, for Calvin, "faith is <u>knowledge</u>."[24] Master Price took as his text I Corinthians 13:12. "These words," he observed appropriately, "sett foorth our knowledge of God." We may know God through "ye light of reason" Such a method "attained to a competent knowledge of God, as appears from many of the Heathens." Such means, however, provided a rather pale and imperfect light when compared:

> to yt great light, ye sunne, wch is faith; wch is ye greatest measure of knowledge wee can attaine unto in ys lyfe.

The standard Reformation definition of faith, based on Hebrews 11:1, followed. "Fayth is ye evidence of thinges not seene."[25] That affirmation thoroughly characterized university theology relative to the concept of faith. Whenever occasion dictated, university theologians defined faith in virtually the same words as found in the epistle to Hebrews. William Whitaker, Fellow of Trinity College and later Master of St. John's College at Cambridge, defined faith in such a manner in a polemical work directed against the Roman Catholics: "the Apostle termeth faith the ground of those things that are hoped for and the evidence of things which are not seen."[26] Once again, in conceptualizing faith according to the Hebrews definition, university theologians closely followed Reformation thinking.[27]

The underlying assumption behind Master Price's contrast between the light of reason and the light of faith is the superiority of faith to reason. Master Price equates faith with the sun as the source of all light. As such it encompasses the lesser and derivative light of reason. Faith incorporates reason; reason does not incorporate faith. Thus, for both epistemological and soteriological purposes, faith supersedes reason. As a consequence, reason necessarily fails to apprehend some of the Christian verities. Some aspects of divine knowledge may be ascertained only upon the foundation of faith. The definition in Hebrews of faith explicitly recognized reason's limitations with its assertion that faith is the acceptance of truths unattainable through reason ("the evidence of things not seen"). The Reformation definition of faith, in short, presumed the superiority of faith to reason.[28]

This theological pattern surfaced in the course of another Oxford theologian's lectures on the trinity. The Fellow began by noting the apparent difficulty of his topic. "Dost thou aske how this may bee," he pondered, "that there should bee three distinct persons in the deitie & yet but one indivisible essence?" The answer, of course, consisted in approaching this difficult doctrine from the perspective of faith. We do not perceive the trinity "wth our corporeall eies" (reason). The theologian identified the dichotomy between reason and faith. Bolstering his argument with the standard Reformation definition, he asserted that faith rather than reason constituted the proper method by which to understand this particular doctrine:

> But wilt thou see it wth the eie of flesh, reason, beefore thou beeleeve it? Thou foolish and perverse man. If I could lay it as a visible object beefore thee that thou mightest see it, I would never exhort thee to beeleeve it for an article of thy faith. Beecause faith is the ground of thinges wch are hoped for & the evidence of thinges wch are not seene. [29]

Reason, in other words, is incapable of perceiving the mystery of the trinity. Faith only may apprehend that particular truth.

It is important to note that faith, as it is used in the above context, means to appropriate unto oneself theological mysteries merely on the foundation of trust in God, exclusive of any external support. As implied in the previous citation, a truth is exempted from verification on the grounds of faith if it may be demonstrated on a rational basis ("If I could lay it as a visible obiect beefore thee that thou mightest see it, I would never exhort thee to beeleeve it for an article of thy faith."). Faith proceedes internally from the heart rather than externally from the head. Its orientation is intrinsic rather than extrensic. Once again, the very syntax of the Hebrews definition restricts the faith conceptualization. Faith is internalized and personalized. Faith might be construed as belief, but only as a very personalized belief as opposed to an intellectual assent to a series of abstractions. It is a personal belief also in God's essential goodness. That is to say, that despite all appearances to the contrary, God will make good on His promises. Accordingly, an unknown Cambridge theologian argued that "they onely have ye Fayth of God & truly Beleeve in God whiche believe him to be true in his promises." [30] Faith is to believe on a personal level, as did Master Shirley, that God intended and planned man's salvation, even as he exiled Adam from the garden.

Given the centrality of the Hebrews definition for the university theology's conceptualization of faith, it is not surprising that university theologians postulated a close connection between faith and the Word. This position also followed naturally from their argument that faith superseded reason relative

to the soteriological question. The aforementioned
Cambridge theologian, for instance, asserted that
those men "hathe ye Fayth of God that Beleeveth ye
worde of God & preferreth it before the wysdome of
man."31 For this Fellow, faith becomes impossible
when divorced from the Word. Scripture constituted
the foundation upon which to build the ediface of
faith. Accordingly, university theologians emphasized
familiarity with scripture as a prerequisite for
faith. Exposure to the Word constituted the first
stage in the ordo salutis. Master Tucker of Exeter
College, Oxford, struck this note during a lecture on
Luke 8:18 ("Take heed then how you hear"). The
theologian began his exegesis with the observation
that this text demonstrated "ye dignity of ye word."
He continued with the argument that that dignity
"appeareth in 3 particulars:"

> 1ly. ye Author of it, God. 2ly. ye
> matter of it, Christ crucified. 3ly. ye
> end of it, ye salvation of our soules.

Given this crucial soteriological importance of
scripture, he devoted the remainder of his lecture to
the importance of proper attentiveness to the Word and
the "daunger of unworthy hearing."32 A year later in
1637 Master Woodhead of University College, Oxford,
developed the same theme while lecturing on the
identical text. That text illustrated that:

> faith in Christ comes by hearing. How
> can they beleeve unles they heare?
> Faith is ye evidence of things not
> seene.

Note, once again, the Hebrews definition of faith. As
with his predecessor Master Tucker, Master Woodhead
admonished his students to hear correctly. He listed
various "wayes of hearinge amise." These included "an
impatient ear;" "a partiall eare" (that is,
inattentiveness); and "ye prejudiciall eare" (that is,
an attitude in opposition to the preacher's).33

Given the epistemological orientation of the
universities, the cause and effect relationship which
their theologians drew between scripture and faith
comes as no surprise. After all, such a relationship
placed soteriological responsibility and, for that
matter, power in the hands of those men entrusted with
scriptural exegesis. That is to say, with university
theologians and their students intended for the

ministry.

Quite evidently, university theologians demonstrated a concern with faith. They also manifested a lively interest with reference to works. That they thought in soteriological terms of works as well as faith may seem at first sight inconsistent. The procedure followed below is, first, to define what university theologians meant by the term and, second, to define the soteriological relationship between faith and works from the vantage point of their respective roles in the <u>ordo salutis.</u> This procedure, hopefully, will rectify somewhat the paradox of a works and faith soteriology.

University theologians strongly asserted the efficacy of a works oriented soteriology. "Learn this you that professe your selves Christians," warned an unknown Oxford theologian,

> bee carefull to shew forth good works. For if your life bee uncleane, your works uncharitable; never tell mee that your faith is good; never say that you doe beeleeve in god; never say that you are Christians; never say that you doe soe much as know god; much lesse beeleeve in him. For to beeleeve in god is to
> love him, & to love him is to keepe his Commandements. Hee that saith that hee knoweth god & keepeth not his Commandements & doth not shewforth good works is a lyar, an hypocrit. an counterfitt & there is no truth in him.[34]

For this particular theologian faith does not necessarily preempt works. Salvation results as much from works (love) as from faith. Indeed, if works are absent ("if your life bee uncleane, your works uncharitable"), then faith is forfeit ("never tell mee that your faith is good") in terms of soteriological efficacy. Moreover, a true epistemology invariably recognizes the importance of works. Man does not truly "knoweth god" until that knowledge bears its proper fruit. A knowledge of God which fails to recognize the necessity of works is a knowledge erroneously presumed. Such a knowledge is a "counterfitt" knowledge devoid of any truth ("there is no truth"). Another Oxford theologian who taught during the same period, around 1600, simply followed

St. James and stated that "faith wthout workes is dead."³⁵ Faith alone will not secure salvation. Works and life (salvation), by contrast, are synonymous. "I would not have you ignorant," continued the theologian,

> that there is a great reward layd up in heaven for them that doe the works of rightuousnes. God is a faithfull rewarder of well doinge.³⁶

University theologians, then, did not emphasize faith at the expense of works.

While the universities recognized the efficacy of works, their theologians carefully distinguished between true and false works. They differentiated between those works which saved and those which damned. Thus, an Oxford theologian warned his students that "superstitious fasts, verball prayers, hypocriticall almes, & whatsoever other fained holines are all to noe ende."³⁷ Such works lacked soteriological worth. Another Oxford theologian expressed a similar concern. "What works doth God soe libberallie reward?" he rhetorically asked.

> Not works of our own invention; not pilgrimages, not creepings to crosse, not superstitious fasts not hypocriticall almes--not fayned holines.³⁸

The problem in either case, revolved around the intentions of the worker. If those intentions were not genuinely religious; that is to say, if they were "hypocriticall" or "fayned," then they were false works. Prescribed and formalized works, such as the pilgrimages and fasts noted above, were suspect. Because they were highly structured, they admitted to a ready facility in terms of their genesis and achievement. A man need not be religiously motivated, for example, in order to participate in an established liturgy ("verball prayers"). Because it failed to provide guarantees of intention, such an attitude towards works prevented soteriological assurance from the perspectives of the individual, the church, and the interaction of both. Moreover, such works were suspect because they emanated from "our own invention" rather than from the authoritative Word.

True works, in contrast, emanated from a structure which in terms of its general authoritative basis, with reference to its liturgical orientation for example, was conducive to the identification of a genuinely religious heart. True works stemmed not from the conceits "of our own invention," but rather from obedience to God as the Word defined hat obedience. "True Christians," observed an unknown Oxford theologian, "worship god in Sinceritie & truth, manifesting their love in true obedience."39 Lecturing on John 14:15 another unknown theologian observed that:

> God's good promises are made to such as walk in iustice and speak rightuous things; to such as refuse the gaine of oppression & shake their hands from receaving bribes; to such as stop their eares from hearing of bloud, & turne their eies from beholding of evill; to such as have innocent hands & pure harts; to such as follow rightuousnes, & love mercie; to such as eschew evill & doe good; in a word to such as love god & keep his Commandments.40

Here, then, are elucidated some specific true works. Refusal to associate with oppression, bribery, and physical assault; innocence; mercy; and obedience to the Tables all signify a proper works orientation. Such works possess soteriological efficacy. The university theologians equated obedience to God with obedience to the Word. Thus, another Oxford theologian chided those men "full of evill works--of fraud & corrupt manners." Such men were "great boasters of faith & beeleefe of god, but smaul workers noe doers of the worde."41 Here he associated false works with disobedience. Another Oxford Fellow developed the same connection during, appropriately enough, a lecture on James 1:27. The apostle spoke of "pure religion," and the theologian defined that phrase from the perspective of works. Most importantly, he defined works from the perspective of the Word. In this scriptural passage, he noted:

> St. James dehorted them from all manner of vice--especiallie from an idle & unprofitable hearinge of god's word. Counseling everie one to continew in the perfect law of libertie, & to bee a doer of the work.42

Presumably, a correct "hearinge of god's word"

transformed a man into "a doer of the work." The "love of god," observed another Oxford theologian, consisted:

> in the keepinge of his word, wch true Christians only streive to doe. There is a great difference beetweene the hearers & doers of his worde.[43]

"True Christians" are saved Christians who are saved through their works; that is, through "love of God." The theologian explicitly tied works, and thus salvation, to the Word. "Doers of his worde" and "the keepinge of his word" constituted the type of activities that resulted in soteriological assurance.

University theologians rather easily identified the types of works sanctioned by scripture. As an initial point of departure, the Pentateuch served quite well. Accordingly, an anonymous Oxford theologian identified true works within the context of the Ten Commandments:

> The matter of good workes are conteyned in the two tables of the Law of god; who only hath absolute authoritie of commandinge & whose law only is the most absolute rule & patterne of all iustice & equitie.

The works commanded here admitted of a threefold division.

> The matter of good workes generallie either respect pietie towards god, or charitie towards our neighbours, or sanctitie in our selves. Those good works wch respects pietie towards god are commanded in the 4 precepts of the first table. Those good works wch respect either charitie towards our neighbours, or charitie in our selves, are particularly conteyned in the 6 precepts of the 2d table. The forme of good works must bee a full & perfect conformitie in all points wth the law of god both according to the outward shew & also according to the inward truth.[44]

Note that this theologian carefully concluded with an admonition against hypocrisy. That is, he emphasized that even works rooted in scripture must proceed from "inward truth." Efficacious works are so because they emanate from a genuinely religious nature. From another perspective this admonition represents another manner of warning against the dangers of improper hearing with reference to scripture, and, as a onsequence, improper doing. One may presume a true works orientation, in other words, only if one has heard rightly and truly the Word. Works worked "according to the inward truth" resulted only from proper hearing.

The New Testament also provided fruitful ground for an inquiry into the specific nature of acceptable works. The theologian noted above who lectured on James 1:27, in his exegesis of that text, closely approximated the definition of true works based on the Ten Commandments. He distinguished between true religion/works and false religion/works:

> The first difference consisteth in the innocencie of the hartes & in the simplicitie of our intention towards god, soe saith our Apostle. Hee doth not say beefore men, because they rather iudge accordinge to the outward shew & appearance, then accordinge unto the inward truth & veritie. The 2d difference consisteth in the charitable helpinge and releevinge of our neighbours, in visitinge the fatherlesse & the widdow in their adversitie. The third in the puritie of incorruption towards himselfe, in keepinge himselfe from the deformities of sinne, from the pollutions of the flesh, from all impuritie, & to use the words of my text, in keepinge himselfe unspotted from the world.[46]

Once again, the dichotomy surfaced between "the outward shew" and the "inward truth." Once again, good works are identified on a threefold level with reference to their relationship to God, their relationship to our fellow man, and their relationship to ourselves. The same theologian rendered a similar judgment concerning the equation of salvation with purity in reference to Paul's epistle to Titus. Paul instructs us there that:

> the grace of god that bringeth salvation unto all men hath appeared, & teacheth us that we should denie ungodlines & worldly lusts; that wee should live soberly, & rightuously, & godly in the present world.

The theologians examined above admonished their students against hypocrisy and insincerity of heart. They defined true works on a strictly individual level with reference to a relative "purity" in personal life. They defined true works on a corporate level with reference to "charity" towards other men. Such works were not the formalized works of pilgrimages and fasts. Rather, they were flexible in their structure. They varied in accordance with the exigencies of the individual and group. As such, they required serious and genuine consideration by the individual regarding the peculiarities of any given works oriented situation. That consideration more readily presumed a sincere religiosity and truthfulness on the part of the worker.

As perhaps well suited a university environment, university theologians emphasized those types of true works which related to "puritie of incorruption." The ideal of a godly life permeated their lectures and sermons. Master Sutton of Christ Church, Oxford, found in his text, Exodus 32:6, ample opportunity to elucidate that ideal. Lecturing his students in September 1635, he noted that "ye wildernes is no place for riot & excesse." Master Sutton continued with identification and admonition against some of the more notable lapses committed by the Israelites in disobedience to God during their odyssey. He noted, for instance, the barriers placed along the path to personal piety by gluttony, idleness, and drunkenness. These three sins, all of which presumably ran rampant in a university community, were interrelated. To become enslaved to one invariably resulted in enslavement to the other two. Master Sutton developed the ramification of each particular sin within the context of his text in which he identified the impure act, and, by implication, the relative pure act. Thus, with reference to gluttony, he noted that whereas the Israelites "should have fasted for Moses' absence they feasted."[47] Lionel Day, Fellow of Balliol College at Oxford, addressed himself to the same subject some forty years earlier in 1595. He lectured topically on the hindrances to personal purity, such as "covetuousness" and "epicurisme," placed before us by Satan. To illustrate his point he provided citations from the Old Testament.[48]

One anonymous Oxford theologian did not content himself with general admonitions, but explicitly accused his students of impurity in their personal lives. "God forbid that any of us shouldbee soe ignorant as to have noe knowledge of god after soe manie yeares of hearinge & preaching of his word," he began. Note, once again, the epistemological and soteriological connotations with reference to the "hearinge & preaching" of the Word. The theologian continued:

> I hope better thinges of you beeloved then soe; & yet I would that you should think itt a point of charitie in mee to bee soe well persuaded of you. Seeinge your manner of livinge deserveth not soe milde a censure; seeinge the great number of drunkards, of swearers, of loyterers, that live in this towne uncorrected; seeinge that great profanation of the Sabothe, spent for the most part in dauncinge & drinkinge & fidlinge unamended; wch argueth if wee may iudge of the tree by the fruits that you have noe knowledge of god.[49]

Master Garland of Magdalene College, Oxford, developed a similar argument in a lecture delivered June 1637. His text, I Peter 5:8 ("Be sober, bee watchfull"), provided an excellent opportunity to admonish his students relative to the obstacles to purity. Master Garland concluded that "my Apostle here in this verse traines men up in military discipline."[50] Here Master Garland struck an image of personal purity from the perspective of Christian warfare. In so doing he echoed the rhetoric of religious humanism. Erasmus, after all, had struck the same military image in Enchiridion, Or Handbook Of A Christian Knight. Indeed, in their teaching pertinent to personal purity the universities closely paralleled the philosophy of piety advocated by Erasmus and other northern humanists.

As the preceding pages illustrate, just as university theologians associated saving faith with the Word, so they linked saving works to the Word. "There wee shall find the true light of knowledg," observed one unknown theologian with respect to scripture:

> If wee stand not knowinge whither to turne our selves, wee shall noe where better than there find good & faithfull counsell. If wee are tempted, & put in danger of salvation, wee have there a most stronge & invincible bulwarke.⁵¹

Be slavation through works or through faith, it is impossible divorced from the Word. In either case the solution to the problem of assurance lay in adherence to the Word. It is the Word which comforts us; which provides us with a "stronge & invincible bulwarke" when we are "in danger of salvation."

Despite this agreement regarding the efficacy of the Word pertinent to salvation, university theologians seemingly impaled themselves on the horns of a soteriological dilemma. They spoke of salvation through faith and salvation through works with facile equanimity. Surely they were cognizant of the dichotomy involved. The question, after all, reverberated throughout the Reformation era. Master Shirley, of Christ Church at Oxford, certainly recognized the apparent paradox. Lecturing o Matthew 7:14 in May 1635 he argued that his text allowed of only one "straight gate" to salvation:

> But now wt this straite way to heaven is, is a matter in controversy. Aske ye Papists, & they will roundly answer, yt good workes are ye onely way. They of ye reformed Churches will tell ye, yt faith in Christ's merits & god's mercy is ye way.⁵²

Master Shirley refused to limit the question's relevance to his contemporaries, but extrapolated its significance throughout the Church's past history:

> Nor is this controversy onely 'teixt ym. Just so did ye Jew & ye Christian differ. Ye Jew stood for ye law of Moses, and justification by it; but ye Xtian beinge sensible of his owne misery, relyas wholly on god's mercy. Nay this is not all. St. Paul & Saint James make these two severall wayes too. St. Paul in Rom: 3:28--yrfore wee conclude yt a man is justifyed by faith,

> without ye deeds of ye law-- & St.
> James, hee is for workes--can faith
> save a man?-- and againe--you see yt by
> workes a man is justifyed & not by
> faith onely--Ch: 2:14, 24. But were it
> as easy to reconcile ye Church of Rome
> with us, & St. Paul with St. James, ye
> controversy would quickly bee ended.[53]

How then, did Master Shirley and other university theologians solve the dilemma? Having taught the efficacy of both faith and works regarding salvation, did they somehow reconcile the two? Or, did they in the final analysis assert the superiority of the one over the other?

To a certain extent, the answers to these questions hinge upon the university teaching regarding the issues of predestination and free will within the context of the *ordo salutis.* A works oriented soteriology usually presupposes free will. Both Luther and Calvin, in contrast, conceptualized faith in terms of predestination. After all, if faith is not a work it must be a gift freely given by God. Accordingly, formulations of predestinarian dogma by university theologians might indicate a soteriological preference slanted towards faith.

As the Reformation progressed, important differences appeared with reference to the precise role played by the various soteriological concepts. For the most part these differences pertained to the place occupied by predestination in the *ordo salutis.* Professor Kendall thoroughly deals with this topic in his study of English Calvinism. Professor Kendall argues that the role played by faith in the salvation process changed from Calvin to Beza. For Calvin, faith preceded repentance and works in the *ordo salutis.* Assurance in our salvation must be sought externally in Christ. Beza reversed this relationship. For Beza, the ground of assurance must be sought elsewhere than in faith in Christ. Soteriological assurance must be sought within ourselves. "Sanctification or good works," notes Professor Kendall with reference to Beza, "is the infallible proof of saving faith."[54] With William Perkins considered as a transitional figure, Professor Kendall argues that English Calvinism more closely followed Beza's soteriology than Calvin's in this regard.[55]

Whatever the truth may be in precise terms relative to Professor Kendall's interpretation of the _ordo salutis_, he has demonstrated to a certainty the flexibility of the _ordo salutis_ in the late sixteenth and early seventeenth centuries. The soteriological situation in this regard was fluid rather than static. Given this reality, it becomes readily apparent that any attempt to discuss the _ordo salutis_ with reference strictly to Anglican and Puritan schools of thought is an exercise in academic self-deception. Scholars consider both Perkins and Baynes, for example, as exemplary models of Puritanism. Professor Kendall proves, however, that their _ordo salutis_ strays far afield from standard definitions of Puritan soteriology.[56] Advancing a similar agrument, Professor John New suggests in his study of the differences separating Anglican from Puritan that questions other than those of the _ordo salutis_ in general and predestination in particular differentiated the two. He maintains that "an exaggerated emphasis on the doctrine of predestination has warped our understanding of religious history."[57] Although perhaps an exaggeration itself, Professor New's argument rightly questions the doctrine's centrality for the late Elizabethan and early Jacobean periods.

With this caveat in mind, it is possible to acknowledge that university theologians on occasion asserted the doctrine of predestination. An unknown Oxford theologian argued that God "did elect & predestinate us unto salvation beefore ether the heavens were streched out or the foundations of the worlde layd." God "doth both will good and doe good" regarding his elect as manifestations of his love and mercy:
> Hee doth will them good by electing & predestinating them unto salvation according to the foreknowledge of his will. Hee hath done them good by redeeminge them by the death of his sonne, by raising them out of the dark of ignorance into the marvelous light of his truth & by iustifying them thorow faith in his sonne. Hee doth them good by sanctifyinge them dayly more & more in this life, & hee will glorifie them in the life to come.[58]

Here the theologian established an _ordo salutis_ which consisted of predestination, justification through faith, sanctification, and salvation.

Another Oxford theologian, Master Yaire, established a similar soteriological progression during a lecture on Romans 6:22. In that particular text Paul "treates of ye state of regeneration wrby a man is changed from nature into grace." Master Yaire continued with an explanation of the process by which this transformation was effected and a description of its consequences:

> In ye change wee have 2 branches: 1ly., God's love to man in freeing him from sin; 2ly., man's duty to God in disposeinge himselfe to his service. The benefitts of this change are likewise two: 1ly., holines in this present lyfe; 2ly., life everlastinge wn this life is ended. 59

Master Yaire assumed predestination with his assertion that through His love God effects the change in man whereby man is freed from sin. As with the previous theologian, sanctification ("holines in this present lyfe") and salvation ("life everlastinge") result. "Faythe is neither in us by Nature nor procured or purchased by oure owne industry or laboure," noted an anonymous Cambridge theologian, "but it is only the guyfte of God & ye worke of ye Holye Gooste."60 Salvation, in other words, originates with God through the action of the Holy Spirit.

Master Simpson of Trinity College, Cambridge, similarly ascribed soteriological responsibility to God in a sermon on John 3:6 delivered in 1617. "This verse consists of a double axiome or Aphorisme," he began,

> Whereof ye former containes in it ye doctrine of our originall corruption shewinge what wee were by Nature; and ye latter containes ye doctrine of our Regeneration shewinge what wee are by Grace. 61

That is to say, the text contrasts man in a state of damnation ("originall corruption") with man in a state of salvation ("Grace"). With regards to the latter, Master Simpson explained that:

> this our newe byrth is ascribed to ye

> Holy Ghost, whoe is ye Spirit of ye Father and ye Sonne, as to ye author and efficient cause thereof. God ye Father by his Sonne, and for his sonne's sake, sends his holy Spirit, ye Spirit of his Sonne, into our harts to regenerate and to sanctifiee us.[62]

Sanctification and salvation ("our newe byrth") result directly from the intervention of God through the Holy Spirit.

Doctor Overall, Fellow of Trinity College at Cambridge during the fifteen-eighties and fifteen-nineties, also argued in favor of predestination as opposed to free will. In an address to the university delivered in St. Mary's Church, he discussed "universality of grace."

> I doubt not but God doth give to all men, & that of his meer grace, some light for the knowledge of sinne, with other notions of grace, & that the end & purpose thereof is, & so should of them be used, to bringe them to repentance & to remove out of yr soules darkness, sinne, death & c. Yet besides this generall grace & conditional will of God, in regard whereof it is truly sayd, that God would have all men to be saved, there is a more speciall Grace of God to be confessed, whereby according to his absolute will & constant purpose, he doth effectually enlighten, call, & bringe some men to repentance, faith, perserverance, & salvation. Wch effectual grace is not universall, but proper to the elect, whom God of his free mercy in Christ hath enternally chosen out of the masse of perdition.[63]

Several things should be noted with reference to Dr. Overall's above statement. The *ordo salutis* here is both similar and different to that characteristic of the theologians discussed above. All men receive from God a "generall grace" which consists primarily of a greater knowledge of God. This knowledge presumably results in a greater proclivity towards repentance. However, God offers not "effectual grace," that is to say, saving grace, to all men. Rather, such grace is offered only to the "eternally chosen." Salvation, in

35

other words, is possible only for those men predestined to that state by God. This "speciall Grace" is endowed with true soteriological worth. It is an "effectual" <u>ordo salutis</u> which originates with predestination and proceeds though repentance, faith, and salvation. Note that Dr. Overall places repentance, which may be construed as works, before faith. William Perkins also accepted predestination. He defined the concept in a treatise on the Apostle's Creed.

> It is a part of the counsell of God, whereby he hath before all times purposed in himselfe to shew mercie on some men, and to passe by others, shewing his iustice on them for the manifestation of the glorie of his own name. [64]

Quite clearly, then, university theologians at times asserted predestinarian doctrine.

Those theologians who endorsed some type of predestination also decidedly emphasized the adverse consequences of the Fall. Master Baker, for example, of Brasenose College at Oxford, argued the point in a lecture on I Corinthians 15:22. "Since Adam's fall we cannot chuse but sin," he asserted, for "hee hath made yt nature in us wch in him was but disobedience." [65] Man after "Adam's fall" lacks, in other words, the freedom of will to pursue disobedience. William Perkins drew a distinction between free will possessed of soteriological efficacy and free will devoid of that quality. After the Fall man retains free will only as it applies to the natural order of mundane affairs. That catastrophic event, however, deprived man of free will with regards to the initial process of salvation. "Though libertie of nature remaine," Perkins noted, "libertie of grace, that is, libertie to will well, is lost, extinguished and abolished by the fall of Adam." [66] Perkins addressed himself to the obvious discrepancy, that the will is both enslaved and free, by developing the image of an imprisoned man who nevertheless enjoys freedom of movement within his cell. "It may be obiected that if the will be in bondage under sinne, it hath lost his libertie quite," Perkins observed rhetorically:

> I answer, not so: for both may stand together. The prisoner though hee have lost a great part of his libertie, yet

> hath he not lost all. For within the prison he may (as he will) either sit, stand, lie, or walke. And though he which is captive to sinne can do nothing but sinne, yet may he in sinning use his libertie, and in the diverse kinds of evils intended, shew the freedome of his wil.[67]

It would seem, then, that predestinarian theology precluded freedom of the will within the soteriological context.

In actual fact, however, predestination and free will were incompatible only to a degree. University theologians in effect narrowly restricted the scope of predestination in the <u>ordo salutis.</u> Predestination necessitated a determined will only in regards to the initial stage of salvation. Once the process of salvation started, free will came into play.

Accordingly, most of the theologians noted above as advocates of predestination also endorsed such a qualified concept of free will. Dr. Overall, for example, characterized the soteriological process as a process from a limited and primarily determined to a free will. "In the beginning of our Conversion," he observed, "the will is not an Agent & worker thereunto, but a meer Patient; & afterward co-worketh with Grace."[68] Predestination and its corollary, 'limited will,' in other words, constitute the operative circumstances governing the genesis of our salvation. Once started, however, the salvation process falls within the venue of free will. In most cases, free will presumably "co-worketh with Grace" to further the soteriological process. However, the possibility remains that abuse of free will might endanger that process. "I am of opinion." resolved Dr. Overall,

> that by reason of free libertie & mutabilitie left unto the will, even under grace, many men after they have received good affections & motions of grace, & thereby begun to believe & live in the Spirit; yet afterwards by yr negligence, lusts, & securitie, do fall away & ende in the flesh. The elect themselves do sometimes fall into such grosse & criminall sinnes, as that thereby they do grievously wound god's

> graces in them, & make yr persons unjust
> & guiltie of God's wrath & Judgment.[69]

To "ende in the flesh" and to become "unjust & guiltie of God's wrath & Judgment" must mean to forfeit, through the faulty use of one's will, salvation.

As previously noted, Master Simpson ascribed original responsibility for the salvation process to God through the operation of the Holy Ghost. Once precipitated through predestination, however, free will influenced that process. Master Simpson explained to his students that:

> a sinner beeinge thus prepared by ye Lawe, ye Gospell of Grace is preached to him. In ye due ministry whereof beeinge seconded with ye holy Sacraments, ye Holy Ghost beegotteth faith in men's harts, wch worketh by Love. Whereby beeinge united unto Christ, and haveinge Fellowship wth him, they obtaine remission of their sinnes through his name, and receive from him ye quickeninge vertue of ye Spirit, by wch the flesh wth ye lusts therof beeinge mortified, they are Regenerate into a newe life. Wherein they have both will and power to bringe forth fruites of thankfullness to God.[70]

Once the "Holy Ghost beegotteth faith" the will is freed to participate in the salvation process. The *ordo salutis* is a state characterized by a free will producing good works ("will and power to bringe forth fruites of thankfullness"). Similarly, Perkins argued that while predestination initiated the salvation process, it freed the will relative to that process. "The will hath power to will," wrote Perkins of man in a state of salvation, "partly that which is good, and partly that which is evil, as daily experience declareth in the lives of iust men."[71] With reference to the issue of predestination and free will, university theologians taught that God, in effect, decided whether or not man would be free to save himself.

Both predestination and free will, then, played an efficacious role in the salvation process. Since faith constitutes the sole criteria in predestinarian soteriology, and since an emphasis upon free will invariably implies a works oriented soteriology, it follows that university theologians placed their soteriology within the context of both faith and works. Neither faith alone nor works alone will secure assurance of salvation. Such assurance results only when faith is wed to works. Accordingly, the <u>ordu salutis</u> for most university theologians consisted of an initial and partial predestination, works/faith (or faith/works), followed by sanctification and assurance of salvation.

In his exegesis on Titus 3:8, for example, one unknown Oxford theologian told his students that "the Apostle Paul doth soe ioyne faith & works together; that faith goeinge beefore, good works must follow after." A "true & lively faith," he continued, "will shewforth good works; wthout wch wee neither glorifie god, nor give good example unto men, nor have true iustification of our selves."; What is quite clear here is that the theologian equated true and saving faith with works. Unless works were joined to faith, justification, and thus salvation itself, is impossible. Another anonymous Oxford theologian asserted the arugement in similar terms. "Faith wthout works is noe faith," he observed, "it is a dead faith wch doth not iustifie."73 Professor Lake discusses at some length William Whitaker's soteriology. He identifies Whitaker as a predestinarian theologian.74 Yet, he also recognizes that Whitaker's predestinarian views did not preclude an assimilation of the works and faith polarities. "For Whitaker," he observes, "good works were necessary for salvation. . . a faith devoid of works was no true faith."75 Professor Lake characterizes the soteriology of George Estye, Fellow of Caius College at Cambridge between 1584 and 1600, to the same effect. As the following citation from one of his lectures indicates, Estye appoached the problem of assurance from the perspective of a working faith as opposed to an idle faith:

> Faith is such a thing as cannot suffer a man to be idle. Here we may learn whether the examination which a man hath of himself is a true examination. If the man do not labour to go forward to increase his faith it is an evident token though he seem to himself to have faith and to examine himself rightly yet he doth it not as he should do. Shall his faith save him, as if he should say

> shall such a faith which maketh him idle save him, surely it is so far from saving him that it is the readiest way to bring him to condemnation. The chiefest thing to be learned is that we always seek and labour for such a faith which may not make us idle but which may bring forth sweet and plentiful fruits which are good works and actions done according to the will of God.[76]

Master Shirley, cited above as one who identified the apparent dilemma between faith and works, reached a similar conclusion with regards to the respective roles of faith and works. He "distinguishes a 2fold faith,"

> 1ly., a bare, livelesse, false faith. 2ly., a true & livieinge faith. Ys is yt wch justifyes a man. By workes a man is justifyed; yt is, by a workeinge faith.[77]

Justification, and therein salvation, result only when works and faith are joined together in "a workeinge faith."[78]

John Bunyan admonished his generation that at the judgment they would not only answer for their faith ("Did you believe?"), but for their works ("Were you Doers, or Talkers only.") as well. A half century annd more before, university theologians posed the same question. They answered it, to a significant degree, in identical fashion.

NOTES

[1] John Bunyan, *The Pilgrim's Progress from this World to that which is to come* (London: Nath. Ponder, 1678). For the subsequent quote cited above, see the entry in the *Dictionary of National Biography.*

[2] London, Bristish Library, Sloane MSS, 227, p. 6.

[3] It almost goes without saying that scholars have recognized and emphasized the importance of soteriological questions in general and the issue of faith opposed to works in particular relative to the theological history of the fifteenth through the seventeenth centuries. For a good, though somewhat biased, synopsis see Alan P. F. Sell, *The Great Debate: Calvinism, Arminianism And Salvation* (Grand Rapids, Michigan: Baker Book House, 1982). Luther tended to pose the soteriological question in terms of a dichotomy between faith and reason. For some of the relevant literature see Heinrich Bornkamm, 'Faith and Reason in the Thought of Erasmus and Luther,' in *Religion and Culture: Essays in Honor of Paul Tillich* ed. by Walter Leibrecht (NY: Harper & Brothers, 1959); Brian A. Gerrish, *Grace and Reason: A Study in the Theology of Luther* (NY: Oxford University Press, 1962); and Gordon Rupp, *The Righteousness of God* (London: Hodder & Stoughton, 1953). For Calvin, see Emil Brunner, *Revelation and Reason: The Christian Doctrine of Faith and Knowledge* (Philadelphia: The Westminster Press, 1946) and Francis Wendel, *Calvin: Sources et Evolution de sa Pensee Religieuse* (Paris: Universitaires de France, 1950). For the literature pertinent to England, see e.g., Norman Pettit, *The Heart Prepared: Grace and Conversion in Puritan Spiritual Life* (New Haven: Yale University Press, 1966) and Rosalie L. Colie, *Light And Enlightenment: A Study Of The Cambridge Platonists And The Dutch Arminians* (Cambridge: The University Press, 1957).

[4] Peter Lake, *Moderate Puritans And The Elizabethan Church* (Cambridge: Cambridge University Press, 1982), p. 280. Professor Lake continues with the pertinent observation that "the false choice of either a rigidly defined, party-based conflict or opposition, or a conflict-free consensus, has to be refused." Ibid.

5 London, British Library, Sloane MSS, 227, p. 74.

6 Cited in Lake, <u>Moderate Puritans,</u> p. 158.

7 London, British Library, Sloane MSS, 227, pp. 73 and 74.

8 Ibid., p. 72

9 Ibid.

10 In the course of developing his thesis with respect to Laurence Chaderton's response to the problems posed in the wake of the Hampton court conference, Professor Lake notes Chaderton's thoughts relative to the question of who shall determine the expediency of questionalbe ceremonies. Writing to Ezekiel Culverwell in 1608, Chaderton argued that only ministers possessed of the "spirit of true spirituality" should decide the issue. That is to say, the minister scholars should determine the matter. As Professor Lake aptly concludes with reference to this point, "it was the godly learned clergy of the type produced by Emmanuel College who were to judge." See Lake, <u>Moderate Puritans</u>, pp. 257 and 258.

11 London, British Library, Sloane MSS, 227, p. 6. In erecting their soteriology upon the foundation of the knowledge of God, university theologians closely approximated Calvin's thought. For a discussion of Calvin's teaching on this subject, see Edward A. Dowe;y, Jr., <u>The Knowledge Of God In Calvin's Theology</u> (NY: Columbia University Press, 1952). "It is no accident that the <u>Institutes,</u> from the first edition to the last, opens with the category of knowledge," Dowey observes. "Calvin is here a kind of Kant, an epistemologist not a metaphysician, with reference to both God and the world." See p. 8.

12 London, British Library, Sloane MSS, 227, p. 55.

13 Ibid.

14 Ibid., pp. 55 and 56.

15 For a thorough discussion of this polarity within Luther's theology, see John Dillenberger, <u>God Hidden and Revealed: The interpretation of Luther's deus absconditus and its significance for religious thought</u> (Philadelphia: Muhlenberg Press,

1953). See also Gerhard Ebeling, *Luther: An Introduction to his Thought* (Philadelphia: Fortress Press, 1964), pp. 25 and 229-237. The distinction between *deus absconditus* and *deus revelatus* also characterized Calvin's thought. For a discussion of it's importance, see T.H. Parker, *Calvin's Doctine Of The Knowledge Of God* (Grand Rapids, Michigan: Wm. B. Eerdmans Publishing Company, 1952). Parker argues that the concept of *deus absconditus* "plays, indeed, a necessary part in Calvin's doctrine of revelation and in his soteriology." See pp. 11 and 12.

[16] London, British Library, Sloane MSS, 227, p. 53.

[17] Oxford, Bodleian Library, MS.Eng.th.f.7, p. 39.

[18] Ibid., p. 12.

[19] Ibid., p. 7.

[20] Ibid., p. 39.

[21] Ibid.

[22] London, British Library, Sloane MSS, 227, p. 60.

[23] Oxford, Bodleian Library, MS.Eng.th.f.7, p. 105.

[24] R. T. Kendall, *Calvin And English Calvinism to 1649* (Oxford: Oxford University Press, 1979), p. 19.

[25] Oxford, Bodleian Library, MS.Eng.th.f.7, pp. 35 and 36.

[26] William Whitaker, *An Answer To The Ten Reasons Of Edmund Campion The Jesuit* (London: 1606), pp. 234 and 235.

[27] Luther's correlation of faith with Hebrews 11:1 explicitly and implicitly manifests itself throughout his work. For example, "Faith concerns itself with matters that are not seen (Heb. 11:1). In order that there may be room for faith, it is necessary that all that is believed by hidden; but these matters cannot be hidden more deeply than when they, as it appears to us, are the very opposite of what we feel and experience." Please note that, in this passage, Luther places faith within the context of *deus absconditus*. This placement follows naturally from the Hebrews definition. See *Luther's Works:* Weimar

Edition, vol. 18, p. 633.

[28] The superiority of faith to reason in spiritual matters is the conclusion reached by Professor Gerrish in _Grace And Reason._ Gerrish identifies the dichotomy in Luther's thought relative to the role played by reason _coram mundo_ and reason's role _coram deo_. As a generalization, reason has a legitimate concern only with the former. It is impotent when applied to the latter. See p. 10. The only exception is the limited role _coram deo_ played by reason in a regenerated state _post fidem_. See p. 17.

[29] London, British Library, Sloane MSS, 227, p. 57.

[30] Cambridge, University Library, MS. Gg.1.29, fol. 4a.

[31] Ibid., fol. 3b.

[32] Oxford, Bodleian Library, MS.Eng.th.f.7, pp. 26 and 27.

[33] Ibid., p. 136.

[34] London, British Library, Sloane MSS 227. p. 48.

[35] Ibid., p. 75. The scriptural citation is, of course, from James 2:26.

[36] Ibid.

[37] Ibid., p. 75.

[38] Ibid., p. 105.

[39] Ibid., p. 5.

[40] Ibid., p. 9.

[41] Ibid., p. 48.

[42] Ibid., p. 70.

[43] Ibid., p. 23.

[44] Ibid., p. 49.

[45] Ibid., p. 76.

[46] Ibid., p. 75.

[47] Oxford, Bodleian Library, MS.Eng.th.f.7, pp. 4 and 5.

[48] Oxford, Bodleian Library, MS.ADD.A.115, p. 59.

[49] London, British Library, Sloane MSS, 227, p. 54.

[50] Oxford, Bodleian Library, MS.Eng.th.f.7, p. 138.

[51] London, British Library, Sloane MSS, 227, p. 5.

[52] Oxford, Bodleian Library, MS.Eng.th.f.7, p. 106.

[53] Ibid.

[54] Kendall, _Calvin And English Calvinism To 1649,_ pp. 26, 24, 29, 32, and 33. Professor Kendal observes that for Beza the ordo salutis took the form of a "practical syllogism" in which "all who have the effects have faith; but I have the effects, therefore (the infallible conclusion) I have faith." See p. 33.

[55] Ibid. For Perkins see chapter 4, "William Perkins's Doctrine of Faith," and chapter 5, "William Perkins's Doctrine of Temporary Faith," in general and, in particular, p. 61. With regards to subsequent English Calvinists see, for example, his section on Paul Baynes (Fellow of Christ's College at Cambridge between 1600 and 1604 and successor to Perkins as lecturer at Great St. Andrews from 1602 until subdued for non-subscription in 1607), pp. 94-102 in general and, in particular, p. 99.

[56] Thus, Professor Kendall, after reviewing the academic confusion relative to the term 'Puritan,' states: "While there is merit in calling some of the divines of this book 'Puritan,' the present study regards the term generally as not very useful. "See p. 6.

[57] John F. H. New, _Anglican And Puritan: The Basis Of Their Opposition, 1558-1640_ (Stanford: Stanford University Press, 1964), pp. 17 and 18.

[58] London, British Library, Sloane MSS, 227, p. 8.

[59] Oxford, Bodleian Library, MS.Eng.th.f.7, p. 130.

[60] Cambridge, University Library, MS.Gg.1.29, fol. 4b.

[61] Cambridge, University Library, MS.Ff.5.25, "A Sermon preached to his Majestye at Roiston by Mr. Simpson, Fellow of Trinitye Colledge in Cambridge, 1617," p. 83.

[62] Ibid.

[63] Cambridge, University Library, MS.Mm.1.37, "Orationes et scripta quaedam Joannis Overall," p. 341.

[64] William Perkins, *An Exposition Of The Symbole or Creede of the Apostles, according to the tenour of the Scripture, and the consent of Orthodoxe Fathers of the Church* printed in *The Works Of That Famous and Worthie Minister of Christ, in the University of Cambridge, M.W. Perkins* (Cambridge: John Legat, 1603), p. 333.

[65] Oxford, Bodleian Library, MS. Eng.th.f.7, p. 108.

[66] William Perkins, *A Treatise Of God's Free Grace And Man's Free-Will* in *The Works,* p. 880.

[67] Ibid., p. 882.

[68] Cambridge, University Library, MS.Mm.1.37, p. 34.

[69] Ibid., p. 343.

[70] Oxford, Bodleian Library, MS.Eng.th.f.7, p. 84.

[71] Perkins, *Treatise Of God's Free Grace,* p. 888.

[72] London, British Library, Sloane MSS, 227, p. 48.

[73] Ibid., p. 76.

[74] Lake, *Moderate Puritans,* pp. 104-106

[75] Ibid., pp. 98 and 99.

[76] Ibid., pp. 159 and 160.

[77] Oxford, Bodleian Library, MS.Eng.th.f.7, p. 106.

[78] Admittedly, the response to the soteriological problem by university theologians as I have presented it is somewhat ambiguous. Ambiguity, however, is not

necessarily inconsistent with truth. In contrast to the political context of European universities, which became increasingly rigid in their dogmatic stance during the late sixteenth and early seventeenth centuries, the English universities remained relatively relaxed in their political sturucture. As we shall see in a later chapter, they were less willing, and also less able, to impose doctrinal formulas on their theologians. As a result, their soteriology remained somewhat amorphous. I owe this insight to a conversation with Professor James Kittelson of Ohio State University. Professor Kittelson has noted the doctrinal rigidily, which characterized theology faculties on the continent. See, e.g., his "Marbach vs. Zanchi: The Resolution of Controversy in late Reformation Strasbourg," The Sixteenth Century Journal, 8 (1977), 31-44.

Chapter III

THE CALVILNIST CONCEPT OF THE TRUE CHURCH: ITS IMPACT ON THE UNIVERSITY ECCLESIOLOGY

In late February of 1579 William Cole, the president of Oxford's Corpus Christi College, wrote a despondent letter to Rodolph Gualter of Zurich, an old friend from the days of the Marian exile. After consoling Gualter on the death of his son, Cole sketched a rather bleak picture of the Puritan situation in England. Of those Marian exiles who had sojourned with him in Zurich, "I have nothing to write, except that out of so many scarcely five are now remaining." Regarding "the state of religion throughout all England," he observed that it remained the same as at Elizabeth's accession. "There is no change whatever."[1] He need not have painted so pessimistic a picture. Although the Elizabethan establishment, as such, repudiated the concept of the true church as defined by Calvinism, English Calvinists attempted with some success surreptitiously to graft that ecclesiology onto the Anglican Church. Both the prophesyings of the fifteenth seventies and the more structured classis movement of the fifteen eighties primarily addressed themselves to that attempt. Although William Cole apparently never participated in the movement, a classis existed at Oxford as well as at her sister university at Cambridge throughout the decade. Indeed, the classis movement centered at the universities and London. The preoccupation with Calvinist ecclesiology among university classis members was not merely academic. Were that ecclesiology to be implemented, the focus of power within the church would shift from the somewhat Erastian Elizabethan establishment to the universities. As the focal points of the classis movement, the universities--especially and specifically the Puritan element therein as ecclesiastically defined--expected to become, given this transformation, the focal point of the church.

Scholars of Elizabethan puritanism have remained almost as oblivious as William Cole to the Classis movement within the universities. Indeed, they have paid only scant attention to the classis movement as a whole. They have added little to our understanding since R.G. Usher's preface to his edition of the Dedham minutes published early this century.

Subsequently, M.M. Knappen mentioned the classis movement in his *Tudor Puritanism,* but he considered the classes only insofar as they intruded into his narrative of the political fortunes of puritansim. Consequently, he offered no evaluation of the intrinsic importance of the classes. A. F. Scott Pearson discussed the classis movement in a similar manner in his biography of Thomas Cartwright. He concentrated on the Puritan efforts in Parliament, and gave the classes only peripheral attention. To some extent recent scholarship has redressed this deficiency. Patrick Collinson, in *The Elizabethan Puritan Movement,* more thoroughly investigated the classis movement. However, he considered the classes neither in their university context nor in terms of their relationship to Calvinist ecclesiology. Finally, in the only substantial study of Tudor religion at the universities, *Reformation And Reaction In Tudor Cambridge,* H.C. Porter paid the classes only cursory consideration. He focused on its impact on university politics.[2]

Scholars have addressed themselves primarily to the ramifications of the classis movement in the political sphere. Consequently, they have failed to appreciate its inherent importance as a religious phenomenon. This neglect is unfortunate because a closer examination of the classis movement reveals the extent to which the Calvinist concept of the true church influenced Puritan thought. Moreover, this tendency to interpret the classis movement simply as an adjunct to the Puritan parliamentary offensive ignores its independent institutional identity. That identity, moreover, evolved largely within the university context. The following analysis attempts to rectify these deficiencies. Accordingly, it begins with a discussion of the classis movement in terms of its relationship to Calvinist ecclesiology and then proceeds to an investigation of its role within the institutional framework of the universities. More particularly, four basic questions need to be answered. First, how did the English Puritans define a true church; in other words, what was their ecclesiology? Secondly, how important was the concept of discipline in that ecclesiology? Thirdly, how did the new ecclesiology find expression in the classis movement? And, finally, how deeply did the classis movement penetrate into university life?

As demonstrated in the previous chapter, it is an erroneous asumption to equate Calvinism/Puritanism exclusively with a predestinarian theology. Substantial agreement existed within the university community with reference to soteriological questions. A Puritan as opposed to an Anglican soteriology simply did not exist. This chapter contends that ecclesiological differences, rather than soteriological, more accurately characterized the conflict between Anglican and Puritan. Beginning with the Marian exile in 1554 and continuing through the classis movement of the fifteen eighties, English Puritans confronted their problems and their antagonists from the Calvinist perspective of the attributes of a true church.

The complex and diffuse components of ecclesiology at first sight defy classification, but essentially an ecclesiology comprehends the distinguishing characteristics of a true church.³ For Luther, as for Calvin and most other early Reformers, two characteristics defined the true church. These marks were the proper administration of the Word and the sacraments.⁴ In his On The Councils and the Church, for example, Luther began with seven marks of the true church, but ended with the two *notae* of the Word and the sacraments. The "distinguishing marks of the church," noted Calvin, are "the preaching of the Word and the observance of the sacraments".⁵ As the Reformation progressed, however, it became increasingly preoccupied with what Tadataka Maruyama, in his study of Bexa's ecclesiology, labelled the problem of "how the church is internally reformed and with what kind of polity and ministerial order it is governed."⁶ Consequently, Calvinsts added to Calvin's distinguishing marks the requirement of sound discipline. Indeed, discipline became the most important attribute of the church. Beza and Bucer occupied the most important positions in this development. Bucer, for example, bluntly states that "where there is no discipline and excommunication there is no Church."⁷ Martyr, Viret, Zanchius, and others contributed as well. This difference should not be over-emphasized. Calvin's abiding concern with discipline manifested itself both in the Institutes Of The Christian Religion and in the Consistory.⁸ Nevertheless, it indicates the increased importance that ecclesiastical obedience held for his progeny.

Some scholars tend to conceptualize Reformation ecclesiology around the polarity of the visible/invisible churches. Consequently, they tend to identify separatism as the only ecclesiological alternative to mainstream Puritanism. They fail to recognize that the classis movement postulated another ecclesiology based on the notae of the true church. An excellent example of this fallacy may be found in Edmund S. Morgan's Visible Saints: The History of a Puritan Idea. Morgan's ecclesiological typology rests not upon the attributes of the true church, but upon the dichotomy between the visible and invisible churches. Mainstream Puritans, according to Professor Morgan, recognized that the visible and invisible churches would never coincide, while Separatists believed the visible church could more closely approximate its pure counterpart. However, Separatists believed the visible church in England so corrupt as to render its transformation impossible.[9] Thus, it was necessary to start fresh.

This sort of ecclesiological polarization ignores the via media of the classis movement. Classis members agreed with Separatists that the visible church should more closely resemble the invisible church. Yet, they remained within the established church because they based their ecclesiology on the characteristics of the true church. Accordingly, they could argue that even though these characteristics were not fully developed in the established church, they existed in rudimentary form and thus could provide the basis for further reformation. Separatists, in contrast, denied that the Anglican church possessed the notae even in rudimentary form. The root of their disagreement with the Puritans stemmed not so much from abstract speculations over the visible/invisible churches as over the possibility of imposing the notae on the Anglican church. Indeed, it may be argued that separatism as well as Puritanism based its ecclesiology on the notae ecclesiae.[10] In political terms relative to the possibility of imposing the notae on the Anglican church, not until the establishment in church and state destroyed the classis movement did separatism become the only alternative.

In ignoring this fact, Professor Morgan distorts the historical reality. As an example, Professor Morgan identifies Francis Johnson, a Fellow of Christ's College at Cambridge during the fifteen eighties, as a Separatist. So he was, but as Professor Lake points out, Johnson became a Separatist only after "the classis movement had ceased to be an effective force in the English Church, constantly holding out the hope of a better tomorrow in the shape of a fully reformed Church of England."¹¹ In other words, Johnson's separatism did not follow from Professor Morgan's typology of visible and invisible churches, but from the lack of a viable alternative after the classis movement collapsed. Thus, this shift to the Separatist camp was the product of expediency rather than adherence to a distinct Separatist ecclesiology.

English Calvinists invariably subscribed to the ecclesiology based on the **notae** rather than that based upon the dichotomy between the visible and invisible churches. The threefold definition of the true church characterized their literary as well as their pragmatic endeavors. For example, the notorious **First Admonition To Parliament,** which embodied the Calvinist program in the early fifteen seventies, declared that "the outwarde markes whereby a true christian church is knowne are preaching of the word purely, ministring of the sacraments sincerely, and ecclesiastical discipline which consisteth in admonition and correction of faults severelie."¹² This definition also graced the correspondence of the period. George Wither, who had studied at Heidelberg when the theology faculty included Zanchius, noted in a letter to the Prince Elector of the Palatinate the "three chief parts of the church." These were "wholesome doctrine, the pure administration of the sacraments, and a rightly constituted ministry, which part also includes a vigorous discipline."¹³

Even among the Marian exiles religious disputes had revolved around the efficacy of this threefold definition. The differences which split the Frankfurt congregation in 1555, for example, arose over a proposed English adaptation of the Genevan order of service.¹⁴ **The Forme of Prayers,** penned primarily by John Knox and William Whittingham, set forth the Calvinist ecclesiology. After a brief reference to the invisible church of the elect, the order proceeded to the visible church which "hathe three tokens, or markes, whereby it may be discerned." The familiar definition followed:

> First, the Worde of God conteyned in the Olde and Newe Testament.... The second is the holy Sacraments, to witt, of Baptisme and the Lordes Supper;.... The third mark of this Church is Ecclesiastical discipline, which standeth in admonition and correction of

fautes. The finall ende wherof is excommunication, by the consent of the Church determyned, if the offender be obstinate."[15]

The order discussed next the four church offices; namely, ministers, elders, teachers, and deacons. With the exception of deacons, it described these from the perspective of the three marks of the church. The minister's responsibilities incorporated all three. He must "distribute faithfully the Word of God, and minister the sacraments sincerely, ever carefull not onely to teache his flock publickly, but also privately to admonishe them." The elders aided the ministers in the disciplinary function of "admonishing, correcting, and ordering" whatever necessary. The teacher's duties related to the first requirement. He ensured "with all diligence that the puritie of the Gospell be not corrupt." To protect the purity of the Word and guarantee gody discipline, the order ordained a Consistory comprised of ministers and elders which met weekly to "diligentlie examine all suche fautes and suspicions as may be espied, not onelie amongest others, but chieflie amongest theym selves." After a brief discussion of the sacraments, the order concluded with a reference to private and public discipline. "If a man committ either in manners or doctrine" ungodly acts, a graduated procedure called for him to be privately admonished by another in the first instance, then in the presence of several people, and finally before the entire congregation. If all these attempts failed, the Consistory excommunicated him. Thus, the order stressed the necessity of discipline throughout its treatment of polity. English Calvinists during the Elizabethan period closely adhered to the blueprint formulated in The Forme of Prayers.

The classis movement, which marked the high tide of Elizabethan Puritanism, epitomized the Calvinist concept of the true church. The classes evolved during the early fifteen eighties out of the prophesyings of the previous decade.[16] In contrast to the prophesyings, which the Elizabethan administration for a time partially sponsored and which to a degree provided for lay participation, the classes met secretly without the approbation of an administration which remained ignorant of their existence until the decade's end. An association of ministers who met regularly to discuss points of doctrine and discipline, the classis in fact acted as a modified

Consistory. It attempted to enforce discipline in both doctrine and behavior.

The Dedham classis demonstrated these concerns throughout its history. That classis stipulated that during its meetings:

> admonition be geven to any of the brethren, ether tutchinge their mynistery, doctryne, or liffe, if any thinge have bene observed or be espied by the brethren necessarely requiringe the same. And that there be...enterpretation of the worde.[17]

It vigorously pursued this goal. At a meeting in December of 1588, for example, a Mr. Stocton asked his colleagues "how he shuld deale with a yong man that had gott into the house of an honest man, he and his wieff being abroade, and bene with his maide in her bed chamber." The classis decided to suspend the man from the Supper "till he saw fruits of repentance." Five years earlier the Dedham classis had sought the judgment of "some godly men in Cambridge" regarding proper behavior on the Sabbath.

Until the Elizabethan administration suppressed them in 1590, approximately one-hundred-and-sixty men distributed among sixteen towns participated in such classis activities. With the possible exception of the London classis, those at Oxford and Cambridge exerted the most influence.[18] Although only meagre sources exist aside from the Dedham minute book, it is possible to document a fairly continuous degree of classis activity relative to the universities throughout the fifteen eighties.

In October 1590 the Vice Chancellor of the University of Cambridge, Thomas Preston, joined John Still, Roger Goade, Edmund Barnett, and John Jegon--all of whom were Fellows of St. John's Colege--in a letter of protest to Lord Burghley, the Chancellor of that university. Apparently, Lord Burghley, obviously a defender of the establishment in church and state, had heard some disquieting rumors regarding the existence of a classis at that college and had questioned the appropriate personnel as to its truth. "None of us did ever heare any fame or speach in the University of any such presbitory, or any such like disorderly meetinge ther before this present," Preston and the others responded, and added their opinion that "we are persuaded there is no such matter."[19] This disclaimer notwithstanding, a classis probably convened at Cambridge as early as 1582 during the commencement act.

In mid-January of 1584 Edward Gellibrand, a Fellow of Magdalene College who apparently organized the Oxford classis, informed his London counterpart, John Field, of the movement's progress in Oxford. He had approached the members of three or four colleges, but had evoked a mixed response. While he found most men "generally favoring reformation" in principle, they faltered "when it commeth to the particular point." On the bright side many "young students of whome there is good hope" wholeheartedly supported his proposal. Later that year during the commencement act at Oxford, a classis debated the question "concerning the proceeding of the Minister in his duety wihout the assistance or tarrying for the Magistrate." In January of 1586 Gellibrand requested Field to send him Walter Travers's revised __Ecclesiasticae Disciplinae.__[20] He later acknowledged its arrival and reported that the classis discussed it. The same year Gellibrand requested Field to send the classis Thomas Cartwright's books as well and inquired when he could journey to London to confer with Cartwright.[21] In June of the following year two members of the Oxford classis, West and Browne, attended a synod at London.[22] Also in 1587 Gellibrand wrote to Field requesting the "iudgment of the godly learned brethren" regarding certain questions relative to the ministry. These included the question of the proper relationship between minister and magistrate discussed several years earlier as well as the question "whether fellowes of Colleges might enter into the ministry, being thereunto bound by their statutes."[23]

A synod held at Cambridge concurrent with the Stourbridge fair in 1588 concluded:

> that the dumbe ministerie was no ministerie, or else no lawfull ministerie: and that the Ministers in their severall charges, should all teach one kind of doctrine, tending to the erecting of the foresaid governement, by Pastors, Doctors, Elders, and Deacons.[24]

The next year at the same time another synod met at St. John's College. The Cambridge brethren included

William Perkins; Thomas Harrison, a Fellow of Trinity College; and Thomas Barbar, also from Trinity College. This synod debated and amended Traver's *Ecclesiasticae Disciplinae* and then subscribed to it. Since 1585 Barbar, along with Gellibrand and Browne from Oxford, had attended the national synods at London. In September of 1590 a London synod, with Barbar and Gellibrand representing their respective universtiy classes, addressed the question of Cartwright's behavior during his forthcoming appearance before the Court of High Commission.

Because it was a secretive, even a conspiratorial, movement, it is extremely difficult to identify classis members or to total the classis membership at the universities. Fifty to sixty participants, the majority of whom were faculty, as a total for both Oxford and Cambridge serves as a conservative guess. However, the influence of the universities in the classis movement far exceeds the circumference of Oxford and Cambridge. As the Dedham inquiry to the Cambridge classis cited above illustrates, the classes tended to look to their university counterparts for leadership. Moreover, given the paramount importance of a learned ministry for English Calvinists, it is safe to assume that a majority of the classis members throughout the realm were products of the universities. There is some hard evidence to support this assertion. In his research into the Dedham classis, for example, Professor Collinson has demonstrated that all but two of the twenty members of the Dedham classis were university graduates.[25] At any event, the examples cited above show the notable degree to which the universities participated in the classis movement.

Cartwright's *A Directory of Church Government* stated that the purpose of classis members "communicating together is, that all things in them may be so directed, both in regard to doctrine, and also of discipline, as by the word of god they ought to be." This work also stipulated that no man be called to the ministry until he had demonstrated that "he will be studious and careful to maintain and preserve wholesome doctrine and ecclesiastical discipline."[26]

This concern with doctrine and discipline permeated the classis movement. It reflected a shift in emphasis regarding the three definitive attributes of the true church.

A preoccupation with the sacraments characterized the early decades of Elizabeth's reign. Thus, the vestiarian controversy during the fifteen sixties centered around alleged improprieties in the administration of the sacraments.27 The Elizabethan establishment, however, defeated the English Calvinists in this conflict. As a result, beginning with Cartwright's lectures on Acts at Cambridge in 1570, English Calvinists shifted the thrust of their attack and concentrated on Anglican abuses regarding the other two *notae* of the true church. Specifically, they criticized the Anglican church because it lacked a learned ministry, and consequently the preaching of true doctrine, as well as proper ecclesiastical discipline.

These concerns preoccupied the university classes. The concern for pure doctrine manifested itself in the Cambridge synod's scathing reference to the Anglican "dumbe ministerie" cited above. It also surfaced in the questions Cambridge sent to the Warwickshire classis. That classis replied to one question "that the faithfull ought not to communicate with unlearned ministers."28 Apparently, the Cambridge classis felt the issue of doctrine to be of sufficient importance to sound out the views of other classes. Note, parenthetically, that university complaints by classis members against "unlearned ministers" and "dumbe" ministers substantiates the argument in the previous chapters of this study that university theologians claimed a monopoly for themselves as minister-scholars. Ministers lacking in university training, by definition, failed to satisfy the requirements relative to pure doctrine. The synod at St. John's College in 1589 demonstrated the classis's efforts to administer discipline. It debated the proper behavior of the godly towards those who "for disobedience to the Consistories admonition" were excommunicated.29

To such problems regarding doctrine and discipline a clandestine organization such as the classis could and did easily address itself. The Elizabethan administration could readily police digressions from the official sacramental policy. For it to identify discrepancies regarding discipline and doctrine posed more difficult problems. It was obvious when a minister appeared in the pulpit in the Genevan gown, but secret meetings, such as the Cambridge synods which were planned to coincide with the Stourbridge fair in order to render detection more difficult, advocating radical change through gradual methods, were difficult to detect. An organized elite could gradually effect a reformation in doctorine and discipline through a subtle indoctrination of the clergy and laymen. The classes fully appreciated this possibility. The London classis, for example, decreed:

> that the Ministers should by little and little, as much as possible they might, draw the Discipline into practise, though they concealed the names, eyther of Presbytery, Edler, or Deacon, making little account of the names for the time, so their offices might secretly be established.[30]

The university classes agreed with London's tactics. In the early fifteen eighties the London classis received:

> from our faithfull brother Maister Gelibrande, a direction of the brethren, concerning the Converting of Churchwardens into Elders, and Collectors into Deacons.[31]

In April of 1588 a classis at Warwickshire returned answers to questions which the Cambridge classis had sent it. Several of these touched the problem of the proper procedure by which to pursue reformation. "Touching the restauration of their Ecclesiasticall discipline," they answered that "it ought to be taught to the people, _data occasione,_ as occasion should serve." They added that "the people are not to be solicitied _publice_ (publickly) to the practise of the discipline _donce_ (till) they be better instructed in the knowledge of it."[32] The Warwickshire classis, in other words, advised their Cambridge brethren to implement their goal through the same gradual indoctrination process adopted by the Oxford and London classes.

Since the classis movement operated furtively, the members of university classes refrained from overt references to their organization. Nevertheless, their university activities to a certain extent reflected their preoccupation with doctrine and discipline. In their public university careers, that is, in their capacities as preachers, teachers, and

59

scholars, they expressed many of the same attitudes which characterized their classis activities.

University theologians vehemently repudiated an ecclesiology based upon the distinction between the visible and invisible churches. "The meaninge of our saviour in this parable," an unknown Oxford Fellow instructed his students regarding Matthew 13 (the parable of the sower),

> bee this: that the elect, the regenerate, the redeemed of the lord as good seede grow up in his seede the church & that the reprobate, the wicked, the hypocrits as tares sowed by the devill live amonge the godlie ever more wronginge & injiringe the goldy as tares doe the growing of wheate. Wch hypocrits covered with the maske of religion cannot by the eie of man bee discerened from the godlie; & therefore in the divine wisedome of god, his ministers his magistrates are not permitted to cutt them off & weede them up. Least in their ignorance the godlie shouldbee punished wth them. But suffereth them both to grow togeather untill harvest, the ende of the world, when hee will command the angells his reapers to gather out of his kingdome all thinges that offend, & them wch doe iniquitie & cast into a furnace of fire, where shalbee weepinge & gnashing of teethe.[33]

Presumably because of our corruption subsequent to the Fall, the "eie of man" is incapable of distinguishing the reprobate from the elect. This fact precludes any differentiation between the visible and invisible churches in temporal time. The theologian continued with the obvious inference against separatism and noted:

> a late error amonge braine sicke reformers, who would have the church soe pure & wthout blemish that they would have noe spot of imperfection appeare in her; & the congregation of the faithful to bee soe cleansed from hypocrits, from adulterers, from covetuous men, from sinners that they would not have a tare

to grow amonge the wheat: & upon a selfe conceite of their owne suernes of their owne holines, will censure & condomne all such as are not favorers of their fonde opinions & doe not consort themselve wth their follies, never looking into their owne harts examinge their owne consciences. Their eies are soe fixed on the doeings of others & themselves soe busie in reforminge other men's manners & in weedinge out of other men in their privat censures that they never reformed themselves, but separate themselves from our church, from Christ's Church.[34]

"The follie of these men is soe eminent," concluded the Fellow with reference to the Separatists, "& this their opinion soe apparently false, that they are rather to bee lamented than confuted."[35]

 Implicit in the above Fellow's argument is the requirement that ecclesiology base itself upon the Word. The parable of the sower indicates that the separatist ecclesiology is wrong because its proposed distinction in temporal time between the visible and invisible churches presupposed an arrogant division into reprobate and elect which Jesus Christ forbade. University theologians tied their ecclesiology to the Word in the same manner and with the same emphasis as that in which they tied their soteriology to the Word. They found nothing in the Word to support an ecclesiology based on the visible/invisible church polarity. "Lett god's word bee our lanterne & light," observed another anonymous Oxford Fellow to his students, "our line & leavell of direction, our candle & compasse to guide & direct us in the true worship of god accordinge to his sacred will revealed in his word."[36] The Word, in other terms, should determine the ecclesiology ("the true worship of god"). In much the same manner Cartwright, as noted above, strictly tied his concept of doctrine and discipline to the Word.

 Although none of the university classis theologians wrote a treatise specifically addressed to the concept of the <u>notae ecclesiae,</u> such as Beza's <u>A Discourse Of The True And Visible Markes Of The Catholique Church,</u> that concept occasionally surfaced in their work. William Perkins's <u>An Exposition Of The Symbol Or Creede Of The</u>

Apostles, for example, stated that "there be three things required to the good estate of a Church: The preaching of the Gospell, the administration of the Sacraments, and the due execution of Discipline according to the worde."[37] In a sermon delivered at St. Mary's Church on I Samuel 4:22 Nathaniel Bernard, another Cambridge theologian, similarly defined the church with reference to the <u>notae.</u> The Ark of the Covenant constituted "the most eminent of all God's ordinances for his publike worship" in that it established the proper ecclesiological framework.

> Itt contained the essentiall notes of a Church. Viz: the word, by ye 2 tables; Sacraments, by the pott of Manna; & discipline, by Aaron's rod.[38]

An Oxford classis member defined the church in similar terms during a disputation at St. Mary's Church (Oxford) in November of 1579. John Reynolds, a Fellow of Corpus Christi College during this period who later achieved prominence as president of his college and participant in the Hampton Court Conference, in the process of defending the proposition that the Roman Church was not the catholic church, stated that:

> a sound and whole Church, the faculties and powers whereof are not imparied, hath fower speciall funcions, as the scriptures shew; namely, to teach the faith, to minister the sacraments, to pray, and practise discipline according to the word of God.[39]

Although he here added the sign of prayer to the standard threefold definition, when he proceeded to elaborate he excluded any further reference to prayer and developed his argument solely with respect to the other three signs.

In the course of their university related activities classis members frequently referred favorably to the Calvinist concept of church government. They wanted to organize the church around the four offices, the duties of which corresponded to their definition of the true church. They argued that the Calvinist model of church polity should be enforced because it most closely approximated the apostolic structure as enunciated in the Word, and the Anglican model scraped because it radically deviated from it. Laurence Chaderton, who became the first Master of Emmanuel College at Cambridge in 1584, developed this theme in a sermon on Romans 12:3-8 delivered that year. He began with the observation that the scriptural pharse "grace given unto me" signified the "gifts which Christ hath given for the perfect building up of his church;" namely, "the office of the pastour, and Doctor, and Elder, and the Deacon." [40] Similarly, with regard to the word "member," he argued that "these members are eyther Doctoures to teache, Pastours to exhort, Elders to rule, or Deacons to distribute." [41] Chaderton devoted the rest of his sermon either to further elucidation of these four offices or to the Anglican church's lamentable divergence from that godly order. The following passage, for example, elaborated upon the elder's responsibilities:

> Edlers are church officers or censors of manners, who by correcting and admonishing the unruly, and incouraging the good, prevented offences, and continued in ruling & governing the church which depended upon them." [42]

Chaderton also noted that the elders suspended the unworthy from the sacraments and, when obstinate, excommunicated them. With regard to the Anglican church, he made his point by developing the familiar image of the church as the bride of Christ. Unfortunately, the Anglican church represented a monstrous parody of nature and as such was a blemished bride. Since she lacked these offices in their apostolic purity, she was as a woman who lacked an arm. Moreover, through additional offices not sanctioned by scripture, she appeared as a woman with three legs. "For, as shee is greeved for the lack of those parts which are wanting," Chaderton observed,

> so shee abhoreth and loatheth such as are abounding: as namely, the callings of Archby. Bysh. Deans. Archdeacons. Decaons. Chancellors. Commissarie. Officials and all such as be rather members & parts of the whore and Strumpet of _Rome_, then of the pure Virgin & Spouse of the immaculate Lambe. [43]

Thomas Brightman, A Fellow of Queen's College at Cambridge, also endorsed the four offices of the church, and again upon the basis of scriptural authority, in his treatise, *A Revelation Of The Revelation.* His references to church government closely approximated the attitudes of Chaderton and the Cambridge classis to which both men belonged. The pastor's duties, for instance, consisted "either in administringe the word & those thinges which usually are wont to accompany it, to wit, the Sacraments & prayers, or els in exercisinge discipline."[44]

The attention to doctrine and discipline which characterized strictly classis activities also characterized the public activites of university theologians. In a thanksgiving sermon before his university in August 1586, for example, Reynolds lamented the fact that:

> by occasion of difficulties and wants, what of men, what of maintenance, her Hignes hath not yet bin able to provide wise and faithful worke men, for the perfit edifying of the house of God with doctrine and discipline.[45]

Thomas Brightman's commentary on Revelation expressed a similar concern. He argued that the text, "I know thy works, that thou are neither cold nor hot," applied to the Anglican church just as much as it had applied to the Laodiceans during the apostolic age. Indeed, the Anglican church was the "counterpaine" of that earlier church. Although the Anglican church possessed the rudiments of sound doctrine, discipline and the other aspects of its "outward regiment is as yet for the greatest parte Antichristian & Romish." Thus, Anglicans "stand iust in the middest betweene cold and hott, betweene the Romish and the Reformed Churches."[46]

Brightman developed at some length his arguments regarding discipline. The procedure for exercising ecclesiastical discipline in the apostolic church closely paralleled, not surprisingly, that of its later Calvinist counterpart. "The general discipline did not in the least manner tolerate men that lived any way deceitably," he wrote,

> but accordinge to the nature of theire crime, it reproved them either privately, or before many, if private admonition had nothinge profited; and then afterwardes it did also keepe them backe from the holy thinges, if they

would not hearken to them that perswaded them to that which was good and right."[47]

Brightman even suggested that discipline constituted the most important component of the church. He argued that the apostolic church "did well and wisely iudge, that otherwise Religion could not be preserved, unles vices were cutt and putt downe with this spirituall sword."[48] He complained that in the Anglican church ecclesiastical courts had usurped the pastor's disciplinary role and demanded that "pastours have the power restored unto them of exercisinge the Censures upon there owne flockes."[49] Chaderton also complained of abuses in ecclesiastical courts, and charged that in such courts "all things for the most part were begunne, continued, and ended for money."[50]

An unknown Oxford Fellow, lecturing his students on Genesis 16, also emphasized the role of discipline. In his exegesis he demonstrated that the strife between Sarai and Hagar figured the strife between the church and heresy. The lesson of the text is the necessity for discipline in order to protect the church against heresy. Accordingly, he noted:

> it appeareth that when the Church shall exercise her ecclesiasticall sensures or the civill magistrate draw out the sword of Justice against hereticks, scismatics, or any vicious and prophane livers, to punish & correct them severlie; it cannot bee called a persecution beecause god figured in Abrahsm, haveinge hard the complaint of his Church figured in Sara, against haughtie presumption, insolencie & tirannie of the Romish Antichrist & his adherents resembled by Hagar as well as all other sinogoges of Satan are, hath given free power unto Sara to punnish Hagar at her owne pleasure; that Hagar may know her selfe & bow downe her stiffe necke unto the yoke of obedience of Christ.[51]

When the Vice Chancellor's Court at Cambridge questioned Nathaniel Bernard for his ecclesiology in general and his concept of discipline in particular, he responded with a reiteration of the definition of the ture church noted above. This time, however, he explicitly argued that discipline constituted a definitive mark of the true church. "I make discipline an essential marke of a setled church," he told the court, "without which it cannott be."

The concern for pure doctrine manifested itself in demands for a learned ministry and castigations of the ignorance of the Anglican ministry. Reynolds criticized "the ignorance of many" Anglican clergy "that are dumbe dogges & cannot barke." [53] In 1578 Chaderton likewise referred to Anglican preachers as "domme dogges." [54] He later elaborated on this theme in his sermons on Romans. The Anglican ministry comprised:

> many ignoraunt men, not onely voide of all skill in the Hebrue, Greeke, and Latin tongues, in Logcike, Rhetorick, and other Artes: but also (which I am ashamed to speake), both voyde of the knowledge of the Doctrine of repentaunce, and also wicked and lewde in life: ... O shamelesse impudency. [55]

That these men asserted the mutual dependence of pure doctrine and a learned ministry followed from their professions as university theologians. They envisioned the universities as seminaries for the education of a learned ministry who would then ensure both pure doctrine and discipline. During a disputation in 1579 Reynolds stated that the university existed so "that it might be a nursurie for Pastours of the Church." He made the same point in an epistle to the Earl of Leicester. "The beginning of Schooles and Universities," he said, "doth shew that they were planted to bee nurseries of Prophets: who, being instructed in the truth of his word, might deliver it to man; and lighten, as starres, the darkenesse of the world with the beames of it." [56]

In such a manner did the public careers of university theologians mirror the concerns of university classes. Moreover, even those univerity theologians (apart from staunch Anglicans) who refused formal allegiance to the classis movement tended to think and teach in terms of the three distinctive notae and their ramifications. The anonymous theologians noted in the previous pages, for example, may or may not have belonged to a university classis. Regardless, they still enunciated the classis and Calvinist ecclesiology. As members of both the university and the classis, those theologians who participated in the classis movement attempted to establish the Calvinist concept of the true church in England in a vigorous manner. Although the Elizabethan administration destroyed the classis movement in 1590, those participants who held university positions, in contrast to non-university classes and their members, remained advantageously placed to propagate the classis ideal and the ecclesiology upon which it was based. As such they effectively lengthened the life span of the classis movement.

Some idea of this influence may be gleaned from the tribute paid to William Perkins by one of his students in 1605. "Whilst he lived he was a shining light to this our church, and being dead is a shining starre in heaven," wrote William Crashawe of his former mentor, "for he turned many to righteousnesse and his doctrine wil shine in Christian Churches whilest the Sunne shineth upon the earth."[57] Perkins must have taught Crashawe well, for the Calvinist ecclesiology surfaced in Crashawe's own activities. For example, in a sermon preached at St. Paul's Cross in 1607, over twenty-five years after the demise of the classis movement, Crashawe defended the Church of England aginst separatism by referring to the notae of Calvinist ecclesiology. "Whereas you say that Wee are wounded incurably, and will not be healed," he rhetorically asked the Brownists:

> wherein are wee deadly or incurably wounded? what fundamentall wound is in our doctrine: what deadly corruption is in our discipline, such as eats out the heart, and life, and being of a Church? What sacrament that Christ ordained do we want? and what have we more than Christ ordained? Tho there were in our Church those wounds you speake of, yet do they not come neere the heart, they bee not deadly, they may blemist the beauty, but endanger not the life of our Church.[58]

The classis movement in general and its university manifestation in particular did much to shape English Calvinism. In the first place, with its definition of the true church based on the Calvinist concept of the notae ecclesiae it offered an ecclesiological alternative to Separatism. Secondly, by emphasizing discipline it distinguished itself sharply from the Anglican perspective, which relegated discipline to ecclesiastical courts.[59] Thirdly, it created in the classis an instrument for the enforcement of discipline and a model for the future church. And finally, by penetrating into both universities it ensured that its ideology would survive into the seventeenth century. Some of the university classis members subsequently enjoyed long and prominent careers. Reynolds still presided over Corpus Christi College at his death in 1607 and Chaderton retained the helm at Emmanuel Colege until 1622. As a final consideration, it should be noted that the tenor of the classis movement and the Calvinist ecclesiology, with their emphasis upon the <u>notae ecclesiae</u> construed within the context of the Word, implied that authority in the church revolve around the minister-scholars at the university who were best qualifed to enunciate the concerns relative to doctrine and discipline.

NOTES

[1] Hastings Robinson, ed., _Zurich Letters_ (Cambridge: Cambridge University Press, 1845), second series, pp. 307 and 308.

[2] R. G. Usher, ed., _The Presbyterian Movement In The Reign Of Queen Elizabeth As Illustrated By The Minute Book Of The Dedham Classis: 1582-1589_ (London: Royal Historical Society, 1905), pp. xvii-xxvii; M.M. Knappen, _Tudor Puritanism: A Chapter In The History Of Idealism_ (Chicago: University of Chicago Press, 1939), pp. 283-297; A. F. Scott Pearson, _Thomas Cartwright And Elizabethan Puritanism_ (Cambridge: Cambridge Press, 1925), pp. 236-272; Patrick Collinson, _The Elizabethan Puritan Movement_ (Berkeley and Los Angeles: University of California Press, 1967); and H. C. Porter, _Reformation And Reaction In Tudor Cambridge_ (Cambridge: Cambridge Press, 1958), pp. 189-201.

[3] Recently, some scholars have paid more attention to the ecclesiological questions posed by the Reformation. See, e.g., Paul D. Davis, _The Church In The Theology Of The Reformers_ (Atlanta: John Knox Press, 1981). Dr. Avis deals particularly with the _notae ecclesiae_ in "Part I: The True Church."

[4] Dr. Avis observes that Luther "progressively narrows down the marks of the Church to the word and sacraments." The supporting citation from Luther reads: "you must not pay regard to external form but to the word and baptism, and the Church must be sought where the sacraments are purely administered, where there are hearers, teachers, and confessors of the word." Ibid., p. 16.

[5] John Calvin, _The Institutes Of The Christian Religion_, 2 vols. (Philadelphia: Westminster Press, 1960), p. 1024.

[6] Tadataka Maruyama, "The Reform Of The True Church: The Ecclesiology of Theodore Beza: (Th.D. diss., Princeton Theological Seminary, 1973), p. 368.

[7] Cited in Avis, _The Church Of The Reformers_, p. 49.

[8] With respect to the _Institutes_, see book 4, chapter 12: "The Discipline Of The Church: Its Chief

Use In Censures And Excommunications." Calvin and his Geneva have, of course, received much attention. For a general assessment of Calvinist ecclesiology see John T. McNeill, "The Church In Sixteenth Century Reformed Theology," The Journal Of Religion, 22 (1942), 251-269. McNeill structures his approach more around the typology of the visible and invisible churches than that of the notae. See also Francois Wendel, Calvin: The Origins And Developments Of His Religious Thought (London: Collins, 1963), chapter 3: "The Organization of the Church in Geneva and the Struggle for Orthodoxy." Generations of scholars have noted the importance of discipline for Calvin. See, for example, Ray C. Petry, "Calvin's Conception Of The 'Communio Sanctorum'" in Church Hisory 5 (1936), 227-238. Petry argued that the effectiveness of the communio sanctorum rested in its purity, and its purity in its discipline. Thus, "when discipline fails, the ommunity disintegrates." For a more recent explanation of Calvinism's emphasis on discipline see Michael Walzer, The Revolution Of The Saints: A Study In The Origins Of Radical Politics (Cambridge: Harvard University Press, 1965). Walzer began his chapter "The New World Of Discipline And Work" with the observaton that Calvinism's preoccupation with discipline was a response to the chaotic social conditions of Tudor Engand. Calvinists perceived discipline as a means of social control.

[9] Edmund S. Morgan, Visible Saints: the History of a Puritan Idea (Ithaca, New York: Cornell University Press, 1963).

[10] One scholar who places separatist ecclesiology within the context of the notae ecclesiae rather than the visible/invisible church polarity is B. R. White, The English Separatist Tradition: From The Marian Martyrs To The Pilgrim Fathers (Oxford: Oxford University Press, 1971). Of the three marks of the true church, Dr. White notes that, for the separatists, "their most urgent desire was to restore the practice of discipline." See p. 32. this made the Separatists remarkably similar to the Puritans. Indeed, as Dr. White points out, the only difference is that the Puritans believed the Anglican church embodied in rudimentary form the notae. Dr. White reaches the appropriate conclusion: "the similarity in ecclesiological convictions between Separatists and the more extreme Puritans made it comparatively easy for individuals to move from one position to the other." See p. 33.

[11] Morgan, *Visible Saints.* See p. 43 for the discussion of Francis Johnson. Peter Lake, "The Dilemma of the Establishment Puritan: the Cambridge Heads and the case of Francis Johnson and Cuthbert Bainbrigg," *Journal Of Ecclesiastical History,* 29 (1978), 34 and 35. With reference to Francis Johnson, Dr. White reaches a similar conclusion. Johnson "had not regarded the move from advanced Puritan to Separtist convictions as involving any great change." See *The English Separatist Tradition,* p. 94. Given the identical ecclesiology with reference to the *notae* of Puritan and Separatist, why should he?

[12] C. E. Douglas and W. H. Frere, eds., *Puritan Manifestoes* (London: 1907), p. 9. For a limited discussion of Calvinist ecclesiology in England see Charles Davis Cremeans, *The Reception of Calvinistic Thought In England* (Urbana, Illinois: University of Illinois Press, 1949), pp. 83-102. Although Cremeans noted the conceptualization based on the threefold definition of the true church, he restricted this observation to his discussion of the *First Admonition To Parliament.* He did not mention it in connection with the other aspects of English Calvinism. Most importantly, he failed to consider the classis movement. Instead, he concentrated on the political activities, notably Cartwright's dispute with Whitgift, of Enlish Calvinists.

[13] *Zurich Letters,* second series, pp. 156-164. For a discussion of Wither see Pearson, *Thomas Cartwright,* pp. 131-133.

[14] For an account of this dispute see William Whittingham, "A Brieff Discours off the troubles begonne at Franckford in Germany Anno Domini 1554," in *The Works Of John Knox,* ed. David Laing, vol. 4 (Edinburgh: 1855).

[15] John Knox and William Whittingham, "The forme of prayers and Ministration of the Sacraments, & c. used in the Englishe Congregation at Geneva and approved by that famous and godly learned man, John Calvyn," in *The Works Of John Knox.* See pp. 172-178 and 204-205 for the citations in this paragraph.

[16] For a synopsis of the prophesyings movement see Collinson, *The Elizabethan Puritan Movement,* pp. 160-200.

[17] Usher, *Minute Book Of The Dedham Clasis.* See respectively, pp. 26, 72, and 30 for the citations in this paragraph.

[18] I do not mean to deny the importance of provincial centers of classis activity. For a discussion of the classis movement in Sussex, for example, see Roger B. Manning, *Religion And Society In Elizabethan Sussex: A Study Of The Enforcement Of The Religious Settlement, 1558-1603* (Bristol: Leicester University Press, 1969), pp. 189-202. Nor did the university classes necessarily control the provincial classes. Rather, the universities are important because they endowed the classis movement with institutional cohesiveness and continuity. Moreover, since the universities provided the clergy throughout the realm, they acted as disseminators of the classis ideal.

[19] London, British Library, Lansdowne MSS, "Lord Burghley's Papers," vol. 63, p. 221.

[20] Richard Bancroft, *Daungerous Positions And Proceedings, published and practised within this Iland of Brytaine, under pretence of Reformation and for the Presbiteriall Discipline* (London: John Wolfe, 1593), pp. 69 and 73-76. As the semiofficial prosecutor of the classis movement, Bancroft had access to depositions and confiscated correspondence.

[20] Richard Bancroft, *A Survey Of The Pretended Holy Discipline* (London: John Wolfe, 1593), p. 375.

[21] Bancroft, *Daungerous Positions,* p. 76.

[22] Bancroft, *Survey,* p. 365.

[23] For this and the remaining citations in this paragraph, see Bancroft, *Daungerous Positions,* pp. 85, 89, 93 and 94.

[24] Collinson, *The Elizabethan Puritan Movement,* p. 225.

[25] Thomas Cartwright, "A Directory of Church Government," printed in *Neal's History Of The Puritans,* vol. 5 (London: R. Cruttwell, 1797), no page.

[26] For a discussion of this conflict see John Henry Primus, _The Vestments Controversy: An Historical Study Of The Earliest Tensions Within The Church Of England In The Reigns Of Edward VI And Elizabeth_ (Kampen: J. H. Kok, 1960). Primus argues that "the vestments issue became the first means of differentiation between those reformers of the church who demanded a radical break with everything associated with Rome, and those who would tolerate vestiges of the past which were seemingly adiaphorus," See pp. xii and xiii.

[27] Bancroft, _Dangerous Positions_, pp. 86 and 87.

[28] Bancroft, _Survey_, pp. 68 and 69.

[29] Bancroft, _Dangerous Positions_, p. 115.

[30] Ibid., p. 86.

[31] Ibid., p. 87.

[32] London, British Library, Sloane MSS, 227, p. 54.

[33] Ibid.

[34] Ibid.

[35] Ibid., p. 72

[36] William Perkins, _An Exposition Of The Creede_, p. 333.

[37] Theodore Beza, _A Discourse Of The True And Visible Markes Of The Catholique Churche_ (London: Robert Walde-grave, 1582). Beza's treatise concentrated on demonstrating that the marks of the Roman Church, such as apostolic succession, were false marks. He argued, in brief, that the marks of the true church were to be discerned only in the writings of the prophets and the apostles.

[38] Cambridge, University Library, MS.Mm.6.54, "The Sermon on I Samuel, 4:22, preached at St. Mary's Cambridge 6 May 1632 by Nath. Bernard," p. 203.

[39] John Reynolds, _The Summe Of The Conference Betweene John Rainoldes And John Hart: Touching The Head And The Faith Of The Church. Whereto Is Annexed A Treatise Intitled, Six Conclusions Touching The Holie Scripture And_

The *Church* (London: George Bishop, 1584), p. 726.

[40] Laurence Chaderton, *A Fruitfull Sermon upon the 3.4.5.6.7. and 8. verses of the 12. Chapter of the Epistle of S. Paul to the Romanes* (London: Robert Walde-grave, 1584), p. 7.

[41] Ibid., p. 39.

[42] Ibid., p. 77.

[43] Ibid., pp. 40-42.

[44] Thomas Brightman, *A Revelation Of The Revelation That Is The Revelation Of St. John Opened Clearly With A Logicall Resolution And Exposition* (Amsterdam, 1615), p. 37. Brightman wrote this work around the turn of the century.

[45] John Reynolds, *A Sermon Upon Part Of The Eighteenth Psalme Preached To The Publike Assembly Of Scholars In The University Of Oxford The Last Day Of August 1586* (Oxford: Joseph Barnes, 1613), p. 11.

[46] Brightman, *Revelation,* p. 132.

[47] Ibid., pp. 38 and 39.

[48] Ibid., p. 150.

[49] Ibid., p. 158.

[50] Laurence Chaderton, *An Excellent And Godly Sermon Most Needefull For This Time Wherein We Live In All Securitie And Sinne To The Great Dishonour Of God And Contempt Of His Holy Word* (London: Christopher Barker, 1578), no page.

[51] London, British Library, Sloane MSS, 227, p. 54.

[52] Cambridge, University Library, MS.Mm.6.54, p. 316.

[53] John Reynolds, *The Prophecie Of Obadiah Opened And Applyed In Sundry Learned And Gracious Sermons Preached At All-Hallowes And St. Maries In Oxford* (Oxford: Joseph Barnes, 1613), pp. 28 and 29.

[54] Chaderton, *Excellent And Godly Sermon,* no page.

55 Chaderton, *A Fruitfull Sermon Upon Romanes*, pp. 34 and 35.

56 Reynolds, *Summe Of The Conference*, pp. 706 and 3.

57 William Crashawe, *Preface* to *Of The Calling Of The Ministerie* in *The Works* (London: Thomas Creede, 1606).

58 William Crashawe, *The Sermon Preached At The Crosse Feb. xiiij. 1607* (London: Edmond Weaver, 1608), p. 27.

59 I owe this observation to Professor Clayton Roberts of Ohio State University.

Chapter IV

UNIVERSITY THEOLOGY WITHIN A POLITICAL CONTEXT

Around 1600 an anonymous Oxford theologian, lecturing to his class on II Kings 17:27, observed "that religion is the only presuersion of common weales." He meant, of course, that a state without true religion necessarily must find itself in grave danger. This theologian, in continuing with his lecture, drove the lesson home by noting the fate of those nations devoid of true religion. "This people inhabitinge Samaria & professing noe religion, but livinge like beasts wthout religion," he observed, "were by god's iudgments made a pray unto beasts & devoured by lyons."[1] This theologian, as well as many others at Oxford and Cambridge, believed it absolutely essential for the state to espouse true religion. Otherwise, the state must succumb before the punishment of a wrathful God. Given this reality, it is not surprising that university theologians concerned themselves with the relationship between church and state. This chapter investigates, on both the theoretical and the practical levels, that concern.

University theologians advocated religious conformity as their ideal. They believed religious pluralism neither possible nor desirable. "Everie man is naturallie desirous to bee of the true religion & to worship the true god," the same unknown Fellow noted above observed for the benefit of his students,

> wch beeing but one, hath but one worship as there is but one god in truthe. Therefore noe Commonwealth ought to admitt a pluralitie of religions.[2]

Diversity of religious thought and behavior subverted the state's security, endangered the soul's salvation, and denigrated the majesty of God. In short, it imperiled both the state and its people. "What means the learned pollititian of this age to make question whether divers religions may not bee established in one & the same commonwealth," the same Fellow rhetorically asked his students.

> Nay what meane some of them in their divelishe wisdome to affirme it good pollicie to leave a libertie of religion unto everie man's choyse, that soe

> everie man might bee of what religion hee best like as if god were to bee worshiped after everie man's owne private fancie, & not accordinge to his will reveled in his word.³

Given this ideal of religious conformity, university theologians and administrators sought to guarantee the safety of their institution against religious diversity. "How necessarye it is that a good conformitye be had & observed in all the members of the Universitye," wrote the Chancellor of the University of Cambridge, Robert Cecil, in 1604 to his Vice Chancellor and the heads of the colleges, "with the avoydinge both of distraction in opinion & diversitye in practice (especially in matter appertayninge to Religion) there is no man of any upright Judgment, but will acknowledge."⁴

That the universities advocated religious conformity as an ideal none who have familiarized themselves with Oxford and Cambridge during the period could doubt. Nor could any one doubt that the universities perceived their role as one of definition and defense relative to that conformity. Religious matters, especially when of a sensitive nature, should be elucidated by the universities. As institutions intimately attuned to religious thought and practise, the universities believed they should participate in the enforcement and, to a certain degree, the formulation of the standard of conformity.

Even the Crown, at times, seemed willing to acquiesce in the universities's concept of their legitimate role concerning religious conformity. Among the "Directions for Preachers" promulgated by the Crown in 1623, for example, was the following article:

> That no Preacher of what Title soever under the Degree of a Bp: or Dean at the least do from henceforth presume to preach in any popular Auditory the deep points of Predestation, election, Reprobation, or of the universality, efficacitie, resistabilitie, or irresistibilitie of god's grace. But leave these Theames to be handled by the learned men; & that moderately & modestly, by way of use & application rather than by way of positive doctrine,

> as being fitter for the schooles & universities, then for simple Auditories.⁵

This article clearly restricted meaningful religious disscusion to the universities and their "learned men." While limiting the universities to a 'moderate & modest' role, the Crown nevertheless admitted the existence and importance of such a role. The universities along with the Crown, then, constituted the enunciators and the protectors of religious conformity. The clergy in general were to conform themselves to the universities.

Both the Crown and the universities, then, recognized that each had a legitimate role to play with reference to religious conformity. Doubts arose, however, with reference to the precise nature of the relationship between the Crown and the universities regarding the enforcement of religious conformity as well as with reference to the specific nature of religious thought and behavior constituting the substance of the ideal of religious conformity. Discussion with regards to these issues failed, at times, to result in any clarity. Agreement between the Crown and the universities relative to some issues failed, at times, to materialize.

The substantive nature of religious conformity appeared patently obvious to Robert Cecil. "And havinge allwayes conceaved," he wrote in the letter noted above,

> that there can be no greater enemye to all good order, then the libertye in the education of yonge gentlemen & schollers, without a dew observation, ether of the Statutes of the universitye, or of ye publicke Constitutions of the Church, for Conformitye; I have resolved not onely out of my particular care & zeale to prevent all sinister interpretation, that our Noble & verteous Societye should give any other then the best example to all good orders, but alsoe in discharge
> of the dutye of that place wch I hold amonge you, most earnestly & affectionately to require you, uppon the receipt of these my letters, presently

> to assemble your selfes together; & take a diligent survey of orderinge of everye the Colledges & Halls in the universitye accordinge to the Statutes of the universitye, the Constitution of the Church, & the orders prescribed in the Booke of Common Prayer, & withall to take present order for the repressing of all libertye heretofore permitted, in publishinge or doinge anythinge to the contrarye, certefyinge me of the Delinquents except they shall assure you of present Reformation.[6]

Here Cecil both defined the substance of religious conformity (adherence to the structure and procedures of the established church as well as acceptance of The Book Of Common Prayer) and explicitly demanded that university officials 'repress' any deviation from that norm. Cecil well recognized that the university played a prominent role in religious affairs; indeed, that it set to a certain extent the pattern for relgious thought and behavior throughout the realm. Accordingly, he enjoined Cambridge to provide "the best example to all good orders."

To a certain extent, and relative to blatant situations, university officials and theologians agreed with the Crown and Cecil's injunction "to take present order for the repressing of all libertye heretofore permitted." In 1586, for example, Ralphe Durden, a student of Pembroke Hall at Cambridge, anticipated somewhat the future course of English history. He advocated religious, and by implication, political, ideas which would still be considered dangerously radical in 1640.[7] The deposition of another student alleged that:

> Durden nameth himself Elias & that Durden said that the 24th of Febr: come twelvemonth England shall have a new Prince & that Prince shall raigne but five months & he shall be a Papist. Then Durden said all that tarys in England shall be damned, except they go with him the sd. Durden to buyld Jerusalem. Durden said that he himself should be Kyinge of the whole Earth.[8]

Presumably Durden founded his claims upon a special revelation rendered unto himself, which allowed him to challenge the established authority in church, state, and university. Quite clearly such an unorthodox viewpoint, and the challenge it represented, could not be tolerated. Durden proposed religious opinions so exaggerated as to ensure instant repudiation by even th most radical of university theologians and administrators. By no stretch of the imagination could Durden's opinions be allowed to fall within the pale of acceptable religious thought and behavior. Accordingly, John Copcot, th Vice Chancellor, wrote Burghley in 1587 to inform the Chancellor that he had imprisoned Durden. He stated as his reson:

> because he named himself Elias & being at liberty would be preaching very disorderly, ...Sins that time he hath written certain papers, & as it seemeth dispersed them abroad; interpreting the Revelation of St. John after his owne fansye, & both in words & writing hathe uttered some dangerous matter.9

According to Vice Chancellor Copcot, Durden's sins numbered two. Copcot obviously concerned himself with the fact that in "interpreting the Revelation of St. John after his own fansye" Durden traduced the authority of the university regarding theology. Furthermore, to allow such a man the liberty to propagate such opinions in such a manner only invited disorder in the state and the church. Accordingly, Copcot urged, as Cecil would over a decade later, that restraints be placed upon such men. Otherwise the authority of the church, the state, and--especially important from Copcot's perspective--the university must be seriously compromised. After all, the universities founded both their epistemology and their soteriology upon their uniquely authoritative character relative to theological issues. To challenge, or worse still to ignore, as Durden ignored, that authoritative character meant, in effect, to challenge their theology and the prominent religious role they envisioned for themselves.

The Crown vehemently prosecuted, especially after the defeat of the classis movement in 1590, any criticism of the established church's ecclesiology within the university community. Thus, John Rudd of Cambridge found himself in trouble in 1596 for criticizing church polity during a sermon delivered the previous year. Among other criticisms, Master Rudd complained "that not the tenth part of the

Ministers of ys our Church of England are able Ministers or Teachers but dumb Dogs."[10] University and Crown officials suspended Master Rudd from his Fellowship, revoked his license to preach, and placed a 40 pound bond on him until he made a suitable "revocation" of his erroneous views before the university assembled at St. Mary's Church. After one unsatisfactory attempt at recantation (Master Rudd at first refused to accept the confession drawn up for him by the administration), he rendered a satisfactory apology and was duly reinstated to his living. Presumably, this judicial proceeding found less support among that segment of the university community favoring a more Calvinist ecclesiology than proceedings of the type directed against Ralphe Durden.

Periodically the Crown addressed itself to the minutia of administrative detail regarding the status of religious conformity at the universities. Crown officials imposed censorship on specific topics if they believed discussion relative to such issues might threaten established authority. In 1578, for instance, Burghley wrote his Vice Chancellor regarding the proposed subjects for a formal disputation at which the queen would be present. "Of the 2 Questions I lyk better the first, *Ad Clementia: magis sit laudanda in Principe quam Serveritas,* then the second, *De Fortuana et Fato,*" he advised, "for this may yeld many reasons impertinent for Christian eares if it be not circumspectly used."[11] The problem with the second question lay in the probability that the debate would encroach upon the subject of predestination. Since Burghley desired to avoid discussion relative to this inflammatory subject, he suggested that the disputation address itself to the safer topic of the relative virtues of sterness and mercy in princes.

University administrators tended to agree with the Crown that questions regarding predestination best be avoided. Twenty years after Burghley's letter noted above, Vice Chancellor John Jegon wrote Archbishop Whitgift to enlist his aid in suppressing discussion relative to that question. "For matters of Scholers may it please your Grace to understand," Jegon began,

> that the Questions of Reprobation & certainty of fayth have lately bene revived, threatinge some disturbance, wch I have hitherto endured for peace's sake, without any publick examina con or

> process therein, to avoyde partaking, hopinge that they will surcese of themselves, or els be less troublesome, by expectinge a further issue, then by urginge a soddaine Conformity. Only I desire, if to your wisedome it seeme meete, your Grace would be pleased by your Letters to advertise our Readers, in Lectures & especially in Determinacons, to maintaine for all matters exactly the Doctrine of the Church of England, established & published by authority. Wch charge from your Grace (I am of opinion) will appease things presente & prevent future trouble in that behalfe.[12]

Jegon obviously believed questions regarding predestination threatened the substance of religious conformity ("the Doctrine of the Church of England, established & published by authority"). Accordingly, he intended to prevent university theologians, and their students, from broaching the subject in either their lectures or disputations ("Determinacons").

In the course of their censorship activities Crown officials monitored published materials as well as those opinions expressed orally during lectures, disputations, or sermons. Archbishop Whitgift, for example, wrote to the university administration at Cambridge in 1586 to complain of a book, __Harmonia Confessiorum Fidei__, recently published at that university. "Theis are therefore to requyre you," he instructed,

> that presently upon receipt hereof you cause the sd: Booke to be stayed from printing any furder & that nothing be done more therein untill you shall receive furder direction from me.[13]

He demanded, in other words, that responsible officials suppress the objectionable book. Archbishop Whitgift continued with a statement of policy relative to university publications.

> And whereas there is order taken by late of the Lordes of the Counsile that from henseforth no Booke shall be imprinted either in London or in any of the

83

> universities, unlesse the same shall be
> allowed & authorized by the Bp: of
> London or my self, I doo lykewise
> requyre you to take speciall care, that
> here- after nothing be imprinted in that
> universitee of Cambridge, but what shall
> be authorized accordingly.[14]

Such measures, presumably, would prevent further infractions relative to conformity.

Years later, in 1622, the Archbishop of Canterbury and other Crown officials sitting in the Privy Council wrote university administrators at Cambridge with regards to the same problem of unauthorized publications. David Paraeus (1548-1622) taught theology at the university at Heidelberg. Upon the basis of his theology, Paraeus advocated resistance to civil authority under certain circumstances. Naturally, the popularity of his publications at the universities troubled the Crown. "An unadvised young man," observed the Privy Council, had preached a "wicked sermon" at Oxford during Lent "tending to no less than sedition, treason & Rebellion against Princes." Upon questioning,"he did shelter himself upon Doctrine taught by Paraeus in his Commentary upon the 13th to the Romans."[15] The Privy Council noted that the establishment in church and state had already pronounced against Paraeus and any others who advocated his theories. Accordinglly, they reiterated their instructions to the effect that:

> every of you that are trusted with the
> care & government of that university,
> being one of the Fountains that water
> the Church & Commonwealth of this
> Realme, to give warning to the Students
> in Divinity there that they take heed
> both of Paraeus & all other hereoticks
> who in their writings doe bend that way.[16]

Instead of Paraeus, continued the Privy Council, students should model their theology after the acceptable ideal of religious conformity. That is to say,

> that they apply themselves to the
> reading of Scriptures, Fathers, &
> Councells of the primitive tymes;
> adjoyning thereunto those thyngs that
> are sett downe by publique authority

> within this Kingdome. As namely the Articles of Religion, Homelies, Catechisms & c: approved by convocation & the writings of many grave Bpps. & other learned men. Wch have written with great Commendation in this Church & out of whome a more exact knowledge of Divinity & truth is to be had, then out of the Books of any late writers who live in Churches & States wch are not so settled as it hath pleased God these are within this Kingdome.[17]

Lest the point be lost, the Privy Council concluded with a demand that administrators purge the university of Paraeus's publications:

> Wee doe further authorise & require you for the better suppression of these dangerous & false assertions of Paraeus, to cause present & diligent search to be made, as well in all Libraries & Studies both publique & private in that university as also amongst the Stationers there, for his aforesaid Booke, & so many of them as shall be found, to see publickly burned in some fit place in detestation of that doctrine.[18]

The Crown, when it felt itself threatened, acknowledged few restraints in its enforcement of religious conformity. The Crown clearly perceived Paraeus's theology as subversive to political stability as well as to religious conformity and moved with vigor to eradicate that danger.

When the Crown most stridently pressed its claim to interpret and enforce religious conformity at the universities, as it did relative to Paraeus's doctrines and Durden's rather unsettled viewpoints, it acted in response to the political implications of such theology. The Crown tended to interfer more in university affairs when administrators, Fellows, and students threatened, in either their doctrine or behavior, political orthodoxy. The Crown, in other words, emphasized the political as opposed to the strictly theological ramifications of religious conformity.

The Crown most adamantly believed that questions of state fell exclusively within its prerogative. As such the universities should not address themselves to political issues. Accordingly, Crown officials attempted to prevent such discussion. In 1578, for example, Burghley conveyed to Dr. Chaderton, the Master of Queens' College at Cambridge, Elizabeth's displeasure regarding such a transgression against her authority at that university. "I perceive the Queenes Majestiee doth mislike," Burghley began,

> that of late such as hath preached afore her in yr: Sermons entred into the discussion of matters properlie appertaininge to matter of goverment rather by privat advise to be imparted to her self or to her Counsell, then in Pulputs to the hearinge of vulgar people, wch are not apte to heare such things. Speciallie therebie to catch lightlie occasions to thinke ether Sinisterlie or doubtfullie of the Head & of her Goverment.[19]

Burghley concluded with his own admonition that in the future Chaderton prevent such behavior within his college.

Some years later in 1616 Rudolph Brownrigg, a Fellow at Pembroke Hall, Cambridge, touched upon political issues in the course of an informal disputation with Master Owen of Clare Hall. Dr. Brownrigg proposed the following questions:

> 1ly. Whether a King breaking fundamental lawes may be opposed? 2ly. What is to be thought of the Noblemen when they opposed King John, making his land feudary to ye Pope?[20]

Regardless of how such questions were answered, their mere proposal constituted a threat to the established political order. Accordingly, the Vice Chancellor's Court investigated this offense and their decision surprised none. "For ye seditious & treacherous questions wch the sd Ms. Brownrigge did propound to Mr. Owen," the Court decreed that the defendant "be censured by his Majty or any of his Majty's Justices or Ministers in that behalf."[21] The punishment imposed by the Crown pursuant to this conviction consisted of temporary deprivation of university positions until the defendant rendered a satisfactory recantation. Dr. Brownrigg tendered the appropriate submission. Accordingly, in March of 1617 the Crown recommended that the university "restore him to his Degree again & to put him in the same state & place he was in before his faults."[22]

In his "Protestation" Dr. Brownrigg not only confessed his error in proposing the questions noted above, but also promised in the future to accept religious conformity "in as full manner as his Majty, the Church of England, & the most learned & authoryzed in yt Question of his Highness's unquestionable supremacy do maintain & teach."[23] That is to say, he accepted the Crown's view of its prerogative ("his Highness's unquestionable supremacy") relative to the question of religious matters. More importantly, Brownrigg promised to "utterly renounce all private opinions of Mr. Calvin or Mr. Beza where in they differ from the doctrine or discipline of ye Church of England."[24] Of interest here is the possibility that Dr. Brownrigg grounded the political ramifications of his theology upon the political philosophy of Calvinism. The Crown, at any rate, apparently believed this to be the case. Since the Crown customarily dictated the substance of such confessions, Brownrigg's apology for the ideas of Calvin and Beza presumably originated with the Crown. The Crown apparently believed that the nature of Brownrigg's proposed questions demonstrated the pernicious influence, with reference to political ideology especially, of those two Reformers.

As will be demonstrated in the following pages, Dr. Brownrigg was not the only university professor to run afoul of the Crown and university administration for expressing religious opinions with dangerous political overtones. In 1628, for example, Master Edwards of Queens's College at Cambridge found himself imprisoned for some remarks spoken during a sermon preached the previous year. According to the complaint, Edwards argued that "it is better to obey God than man." Questioned about this statement by university authorities, Master Edwards hastened to explain that "he desired not to be mistaken, as if he had preached against obedience to Superiors."[25] He went on to clarify that he addressed the question of obedience within the domestic, as opposed to the political, sphere. The text of his sermon substantiates his defense. For example, he urged that those in positions of domestic dependence seek guidance from godly men rather than from their household superiors. "When there arise any doubts" relative to proper behavior, he had urged,

> if thou beest a servant, thou must not go to thy carnal Mr. to inquire of him; if hou beest a Wife, thou must not go to thy Carnal Husband to aske; if thou beest a son, thou must not go to thy Carnal Father; if thou beest a Pupil, thou must not go to thy Carnal Tutor to aske him. But thou must find out a Man in whome the Spirit of God dwells; one that is renewed by Grace & he shall direct thee.[26]

Of course, it would be possible for the congregation to extrapolate this principle into the political sphere. If one should ignore--if necessary--traditional patterns of authority in domestic affairs, in other words, the congregation might conclude that traditional patterns of authority in the political sphere should be repudiated as well. They might conclude that allegiance should be given only to those rulers "in whome the Spirit of God dwells." Presumably, this possibility is what the authorities feared. At any rate, the episode demonstrates that only a tenuous and fragile connection to politics need be necessary for the establishment in church and state to intervene.

Certain elements in Calvinist thought regarding political theory struck the English Crown as dangerously subversive. As the relgious wars engulfed late sixteenth century France, the Calvinist Huguenots developed a theory of political resistance to established authority as a polemical response to the Catholic Guise faction.[27] Among the more prominent of the "Monarchomachs," a pejorative term coined by the Scot, William Barclay, in 1600, were Theodore Beza and Phillip Du Plessis-Mornay. In their respective polemical responses to the St. Bartholomew's Day Massacre, <u>De Jure Magistratum</u> (1574) and <u>Vindicae Contra Tyrannos</u> (1579), they devploped a theological justification for resistance to ungodly and tyrannical kings. In essence, their theory extrapolated covenant theology into the political sphere.[28]

Covenant theology implied that a contractual

relationship existed in this temporal world between ruler and ruled which paralleled in structure a similar relationship between God and the individual sinner as well as between God and nations/religious communities. When the ruler violated fundamental religious precepts, or fundamental political concepts based on such precepts, he violated the covenant between God and that particular nation. Since the well being of any nation depended upon the continuity of its covenant with God, any act which jeopardized that covenant jeopardized the nation's safety. Accordingly, such acts constituted treasonous behavior against both the nation and God. Under such circumstances the people's civic and religious duties coincided to render resistance to such a ruler necessary. Indeed, such resistance became a religious obligation.

Both Beza and Du Plessis-Mornay posited such a dual covenant. Du Plessis-Mornay defined this "twofold covenant" as follows:

> the first, between God, the king, and the people that the people will be God's people; the second, between the king and the people that if he is a proper ruler, he will be obeyed accordingly.[29]

The people or their representatives must resist the king's violation of either covenant. The people "very gravely sin against the Covenant with God," Du Plessis-Mornay warned, "if they do not use force against a king who corrupts God's Law or prevents its restoration."[30] The coronation oath established the second covenant between the king and the people. If the king broke his promise to "rule justly and according to the Law," the people were "released from any obligation."[31] Likewise, Beza argued that if the king broke the coronation oath, the people "are free of their oath."[32] The ancient kingdom of Israel provided for both men the example par excellence of a covenanted community.[33] Such, in brief, was the theory of legitimate resistance to established authority developed by the Monarchomacs. Quite clearly, the Englsh Crown had ample reason to fear the intrusion of such a theory into the university atmosphere.

The Crown's concern that such radical political theories as those which characterized Calvinist Huguenots had permeated English universities closely approximated the truth of the situation. Implicit in Dr. Brownrigg's disputation questions, for example, lay the essential covenant idea of a contractual relationship between ruler and ruled. Merely the syntax of the first question ("Whether a king breaking fundamental laws may be opposed?") predisposed a theory of fundamental law establishing reciprocal obligations and rights which no godly ruler could contradict.

Nathaniel Bernard, Fellow of Emmanuel College at Cambridge, also appeared before the Vice Chancellor's Court. That Court in 1632 addressed itself to Bernard's exegesis of I Samuel 4:22 ("The glory has departed from Israel, for the ark of God has been captured.") noted above in the previous chapter. The text lent itself to allusions to covenant theology. The Court apparently felt some concern on this regard. The fourth article of indictment stated:

> in declaring ye judgment of God against a Nation that departs from the purity of God's worship in his Ordinance, he said these words, or to ye same affect: "If you looke over the Histories of all times you shall never finde that God did bring any general evil upon a nation, as plague or famine, unless that Nation had first departed from the purity of God's worship in his Ordinance." This he sayd once & again with great asservation, bringing therby (as generally was conceived) a Scandall upon our Church, by reason of ye late years of pestilence & famine among us.[34]

Master Bernard, in other words, argued that England had broken her covenant with God and unhappy consequences, such as plague and famine, resulted. As noted in the previous chapter Bernard advocated a Calvinist ecclesiology. Adherence to the Anglican ecclesiology constituted for Bernard a violation of the covenant. The covenant mandated a church modelled after the Calvinist **notae** ("the purity of God's worship"). England's repudiation of the Calvinist structure for a true church had jeopardized the covenant resulting in those manifestations of God's displeasure. As such, the establishment in church and state must be held accountable for this situation. "He spake very bitterly against those that labour to corrupt ye purity of God's ordinance & do what they can to make the glory depart from us," began the fifth article of the indictment:

> Among such, he named those among us, that account reading preaching, & that would justle out preaching by reading, & those Cassanderas among us (wch, sayd he, you know better than I) that hold a possibility of Salvation in ye Church of Rome, & so dishearten many weak ones among us. And those that set up Crucifixes & Altars now a dayes, contrary to ye Law established & in force, & those that bow down towards the Altar, wch to speak in plain English (sayd he) do worship the Altar, & are flat idolaters.35

Here Master Bernard addressed himself to two marks of the true church; namely, the proper preaching of the Word and the correct administration of the sacraments. Because the faults noted above concerning these two marks constituted a violation of the covenant, those who advocated such an erroneous ecclesiology committed an act treasonous to both church and state. Resistance to such acts was necessary. "He added these words or to the same effect," continued the indictment.

> All these are enemies to our Church & State. Yes they are all Traytors & greater Trayters than those who are Traytors to ye King. Treason against the state is greater & worse than Treason against the King. The reason is because the whole is better & of more consequence than any one Member of it, & the end is better than ye meanes. Therefore those Traytors against the State are worse than any Traytors against the King. Against all such Trayters then, let us take up armes (there he made a good long pause), I mean ye armes of ye Church our prayers, desiring God to convert ym all.36

Master Bernard found himself not only deprived of his offices but imprisoned for his infraction. After a suitable recantation, an appearance before the Court of High Commission, and a petition to the Crown--all of which indicate the seriousness with which established authority approached the case--he was pardoned.³⁷

University administrators and theologians then, to conclude this chapter, agreed with the Crown that religious pluralism and diversity in theological thought must be avoided. They tended, however, to express a greater concern when sentiments espousing such pluralism and/or diversity found expression among those, such as Ralphe Durden, who attempted a repudiation of university authority. They also wanted to prevent meaningful discussion, in the sense of potential impact on theological policy, among those men never associated with a university. Their true concern, in other words, pertained to the preservation of their theological monopoly visi-a-vis the nation at large. For its part, the Crown harbored greater animosity towards those within the universities who extrapolated disquieting political concepts from university theology. Theological speculation distressed the establishmnt in church and state much less than political speculation. This is distinction which Master Bernard and others ignored at their peril.

NOTES

[1] London, British Library, Sloane MSS, 227, p. 70.

[2] Ibid.

[3] Ibid., p. 73.

[4] Cambridge, University Library, MS.Mm.1.40, "Copies of letters (most originall) from Lord Burghley, R. earle of Leycester, Sir W. Ralegh, Archbps, Parker, Whitgift, Bancroft, lord North, Sir Edw. Coke, Rob. earl of Salisbury, H. earle of Northampton, & c. taken from a volume of letters in the registrary's office, so mixt and confus'd, that they cannot be reduc't to any tolerable order," p. 382

[5] Cambridge, University Library, MS.Mm.1.38, "Copies of letters & c. that passt during Dr. Jegon's vice-chancellorship ann 1600, 1601," p. 141.

[6] Cambridge, University Library, MS.Mm.1.40, pp. 382 and 383.

[7] For a thorough discussion of the permeation of radical ideas similar to Durden's in the early seventeenth century, see Christopher Hill, The World Turned Upside Down: Radical Ideas during the English Revolution (New York: Viking Press, 1972).

[8] Cambridge, University Library, MS.Mm.2.23, "Trials before the Vicechancellor," p. 27.

[9] Ibid.

[10] For this and other source material pertinent to the case, see ibid., pp. 193-195.

[11] Cambridge, University Library, MS.Mm.1.40, p. 377.

[12] Cambridge, University Library, MS.Mm.1.35, "The copies of diverse Letters from privie Counsaillours & Men of Ho: sent to the Vicechan: & Heads of Coll: there, in the tyme of Dr. Jegon Ans: 1596, 1597, & c," pp. 382 and 383.

[13] Cambridge, University Library, MS.Mm.1.40, p. 351.

[14] Ibid.

[15] Cambridge, University Library, MS.Mm.1.38, p. 262.

[16] Ibid.

[17] Ibid., p. 263. Note that the definition of religious conformity here parallels that given by Robert Cecil in 1604.

[18] Ibid.

[19] Ibid., pp. 352 and 353.

[20] Cambridge, University Library, MS.Mm.2.23, p. 196.

[21] Ibid., p. 197.

[22] Ibid.

[23] Ibid.

[24] Ibid.

[25] Ibid., p. 199.

[26] Ibid.

[27] Scholars have noted well the contributions to political theory by Calvinist Huguenots. See, e.g., Ralph E. Giesey, "The Monarchomach Triumvirs: Hotman, Beza and Mornay, " <u>Bibliotheque D'Humanisme Et Renaissance: Travaux Et Documents,</u> 32 (1970); and Harold J. Laski: Introduction to <u>A Defense of Liberty Against Tyrants: A Translation Of The Vindiciae Contra Tyrannos</u> (London: G. Bell and Sons, 1924). Professor Laski's observations are of particular interest. With respect to Beza, for instance, he notes: "The theory of Calvinist politics is here set forth with perfect clarity. To God alone, it urges, does absolute power belong. Magistrates, indeed, have wide authority, and they cannot be held to account by the people. Nevertheless, when they command something that is incompatible with true religioun, disobedience becomes a duty. And by disobedience, Beza argues, rebellion may, ultimately, be implied." See pp. 24 and 25.

[28] For an explanation of covenant theology, expecially as it appertains to English theology, see

the following: Richard L. Greaves, "The Origins and Early Development of English Covenant Thought," *The Historian,* 31 (1968); Richard L. Greaves, John Knox and the Covenant Tradition," *The Journal Of Ecclesiastical History,* 24 (1973); Jens G. Moller, "The Beginnings of Puritan Covenant Theology," *The Journal Of Ecclesiastical History,* 14 (1963); and John Von Rohr, "Covenant And Assurance: in Early English Puritanism," *Church History,* 34 (1965); and J. Wayne Baker, *Heinrich Bullinger and the Covenant: The Other Reformed Tradition* (Athens, Ohio: Ohio Unversity Press, 1980), p. 166 and following. All of these scholars are in basic agreement regarding the basic components of sixteenth and seventeenth century covenant theology. Greaves, e.g., in his "John Knox and the Covenant Tradition," provides a representative definition of the concept when he writes that "the basic provisions of the covenant--and these were commonly stated by covenant writers--were that God would be the believers' God if they would be his people. From God came grace and goodness; from man, service in body and spirit. God would preserve his elect from damnation; man would refuse to worship other gods." see p. 25.

[29] Julian H. Franklin, ed., *Constitutionalism And Resistance In the Sixteenth Century: Three Treatises By Hotman, Beza & Mornay* (New York: Western Publishing Co., 1969), p. 143.

[30] Ibid., p. 157.

[31] Ibid., p. 181

[32] Ibid., p. 111.

[33] Ibid., pp. 116 and 163.

[34] Cambridge, University Library, MS.Mm.2.23, p. 200.

[35] Ibid.

[36] Ibid., p. 201.

[37] For the relevant documents, see ibid., pp. 202-206.

Chapter V

PURITANISM, REVOLUTION, AND THE UNIVERSITIES

Some of the theological and political ideas circulating within the universities during the late sixteenth and early seventeenth centuries admitted of application, although most often with modifications, to the disruptive climate which characterized England during the revolutionary period. In defining treason with reference to the state rather than the ruler, for instance, Master Bernard introduced a new element into English political theory. Parliament had provided the prevalent and definitive identification of treason in 1352. The statute enacted in that year asserted that treason consisted of those acts that resulted, or were intended to result, in the king's death.[1] Bernard amended that law in that he replaced the king as the focal point of sovereignty with, in effect, a concept of fundamental law based on covenant theology structured around the Calvinist ecclesiology. Treason constituted, for Bernard, acts directed not against the ruler but against this fundamental law; that is to say, against the dual covenant between God and the nation and between the ruler and the ruled in which both ruler and ruled pledged themselves to uphold "the purity of God's worship."

Bernard enunciated this heresy against the ideals of religious and political authority and conformity in 1632. Less than a decade later, his innovation in political theory played a crucial role in the initial stages of the English Revolution. The Puritan/Parliamentary faction provided the opening gambit of that revolution when, during the first month of the Long Parliament, they impeached the Earl of Strafford on the charge of treason. As an adovocate of the policy of "thorough" during the eleven year period of personal rule, Strafford had much to account for in the eyes of the opposition. Accordingly, the first twenty-eight articles of the indictment listed specific instances of his tyranny. The last article of the indictment, however, was the most important. It charged that the accumulative effect of the previous articles constituted treasonous behavior in which Strafford had:

> traiterously endeavored to subvert the Fundamental Laws and Government of the Realms of England and Ireland, and in stead thereof, to introduce an Arbitrary

and Tyrannical Government against Law.[2]

Here is the new definition of treason suggested by Brownrigg and enunciated by Bernard based on the Calvinist theory of legitimate resistance to established authority.[3] Contemporaries quickly recognized the innovation. One observer to the trial noted that an "endeavour to subvert the fundamental laws was a species of constructive treason till then unknown."[4] Although admittedly a biased oberver, Strafford nevertheless was well versed in the law. He too perceived the innovation. "Under favour my Lords I do not conceive," he observed in his own defense, "that there is either Statute-Law or Common-Law that hath declared this, endeavouring to Subvert the Fundamental Lawes, to be High Treason."[5] After a lengthy trial, during which the Puritan/Parliamentary faction discovered that the opposition engendered by this new political theory was so strong as to necessitate a tactical switch in procedure from impeachment to bill of attainder, Parliament convicted and then executed Strafford. In so doing, it vindicated the new definition of treason and the Calvinist theory of legitimate resistance upon which it was founded.

Other aspects of university theology presented themselves as susceptible to radical and revolutionary implications. Paul Christianson, in his **Reformers And Babylon,** discusses the relationship between theology and radical political ideas emergent by 1640. While he refrains from explicit consideration of the university context, some of his comments appertain to the university climate. Eschatological concepts, for example, could serve as something of a springboard for radical political behavior. Mr. Christianson interprets Thomas Brightman in this regard. Brightman's "millenarianism introduced a new, potentially explosive element into English apocalyptic visions," he observes with reference to **A Revelation Of the Revelation,** because "by linking the reformation of the church with a thousand-year rule of the saints on earth, he paved the way for a new political outpouring of the spirit."[6] Obviously, a belief that the final days were approaching placed upon the godly both a new imperative to finsh the process of Reformation and a new confidence that the task could be completed. In so far as univerity theologians discussed eschatology, they contributed to this line of thouht. The Calvinist ecclesiology also served radical ideology. Nathaniel Holmes, who received his D.D. from Oxford in 1637, warned the Long Parliament in 1641 that unless they structured the church in accordance with the criteria of the notae, the godly would find other instruments to implement that ecclesiology.[7] Dr. Holmes's attitude simply represents a re-emergence of the ideals enunciated by the classis movement, although with the addition of radical and revolutionary overtones with reference to the means by which the notae could be implemented.

The question which necessarily must present itself at this juncture regards the extent to which radical political views extrapolated from a 'radical' theology permeated the university community. In short, were the views of Master Bernard and others typical or atypical of most university thought? Some contemporaries thought they were. Almost thirty years after the Long Parliament convened, for example, Thomas Hobbes addressed himself to the English Revolution in his *Behemoth: Or The Long Parliament.* The first "Dialogue" of that work raised the issue of causation. The primary cause of that rebellion, as Hobbes identified it, consisted of an ideology subversive to established authority in church and state which the universities disseminated. "And as the Presbyterians brought with them into their churches their divinity from the universities," Hobbes observed, "so did many of the gentlemen bring their politics from thence into the Parliament."[8] Possessed of a university education, such men questioned their exclusion from the process which formulated and implemented policies governing church and state. "For it is a hard matter for men when they have acquired the learning of the university," Hobbes noted, "to be persuaded that they want any ability requisite for the government of a commonwealth."[9] Instead of protecting and bolstering established authority, the universities intended to supplant that authority. "The Universites have been to this nation as the wooden horse was to the Trojans," wrote Hobbes and "the core of rebellion are the Universiies."[10] With all due respect for Thomas Hobbes, however, the extant sources fail to verify that a majority of university theologians advocated radical political ideas of the type espoused by Master Bernard. Unversity Monarchomachs, in other words, were always a minority (and, in numerical terms, probably an insignificant minority) in the university community.

The fact noted in the previous paragraph, unfortunately, raises something of a dilemma. Master

Bernard's fate notwithstanding, the extent of the Crown's failure to eradicate Monarchomach theory is, I believe, self-evident upon examination of the political ideas which surfaced throughout the nation and especially in Parliament after 1640. Quite clearly, the Puritan/Parliamentary faction founded their ideology upon the concept of legitimate resistance to established authority when that authority had violated the covenants. John F. Wilson has thoroughly investigated the relationship between covenant theology and Puritan political theory as expostulated by Puritan divines before the Long Parliament. The political theory which Professor Wilson describes mirrors exactly that developed by such university theologians as Nathaniel Bernard during the decades previous to the revolution. This correlation is hardly surprising given the fact that the divines discussed by Professor Wilson were almost exclusively the products of the universities.[11] Thus, the problem presents itself. If university Monarchomachs constituted such a diminutive minority, then how is it that university graduates vociferously endorsed their theories after 1640?

The solution to this problem lies in a careful differentiation between Monarchomach political theory based on the covenant and covenant theology devoid of blatant political overtones. While few university theologians endorsed the Monarchomach extrapolations upon covenant theology, they did appropriate--almost without exception--covenant theology itself. God "made wth us a covenant of life & peace," and unknown Oxford theologian told his students,

> wch covenant when our first parents had wilfullie broken by eating the forbidden fruit; & had deserved everlasting death & damnation both they & all their posteritie thorow them; yet such was the aboundence of god's love unto us that then hee made unto us a comfortable promise that the seede of the woman should bruse the serpents head. Wch promise in the fulnes of tyme hee performed by sending his only beegotten sonne into the world to receave the chastisement of our peace & to dye for us.[12]

Once may cite William Perkins as another example of the popularity of covenant theology. Perkins defined the covenant in the following terms:

> God's covenant is his contract with man, concerning life eternal upon certaine conditions. This covenant consisteth of two parts: God's promise to man & Man's promise to God. God's Promise to man, is that, whereby he bindeth himself to man to be his God, if he breake not the condition. Man's promise to god, is that, whereby he voweth his allegiance unto his Lord, and to performe the condition betweene them. Againe, there are two kindes of this covenant. The covenant of workes, and the covenant of grace. 13

The popularity of covenant theology provided a framework around which radical Monarchomach political theory could, at the opportune time, coalesce. University theologians, albeit unwittingly, laid the foundation upon which the ediface of radical political theory could easily be erected during the troubled times following 1640.

The question discussed above relative to the popularity of covenant theology and Monarchomach political theory at the universities presupposes another, perhaps more important, question. Since covenant theology and Monarchomach political theory are usually associated with Calvinism/Puritanism, the logical question must be addressed. How extensive was Calvinism/Puritanism at Oxford and Cambridge during the half-century preceeding the revolution?

Thomas Hobbes thought the 'disease' widespread. Implicit in Hobbes's denunciation is the identification of university theology and politics as, in essence, a Puritan theology and politics. It was as centers of Puritanism that the universities propagated subversive ideology. Subsequent historiography tends to disagree with Hobbes. The contemporary argument asserts, in brief, that Puritanism, which is defined exclusively with reference to Calvinist predestinarian theology, briefly flourished at Oxford and Cambridge during the fifteen eighties only to find itself vanquished by a resurgent and triumphant Anglicanism, defined in Arminian terms, by the turn of the century.

Two of the most prominent historians of the later

sixteenth and early seventeenth century university, H. C. Porter and Mark H. Curtis, argue this interpretation. Professor Curtis, for example, defines university Puritans in terms of "their intense belief in the reformed doctrine of justification by faith alone--especially the doctrine of predestination" [14] He argues that Puritanism so defined did not survive the celebrated cases of William Barrett and Peter Baro during the fifteen-nineties. William Barrett, a Fellow of Caius College at Cambridge, deviated from the doctrine of predestination in the course of a sermon delivered in 1595. University and Crown officials intervened with the purpose of eradicating such viewpoints. The consequent Lambeth Articles officially endorsed the doctrine of predestination. The Crown also stipulated that nothing contrary to the articles were to be advocated within the universities. The responsible officials, however, never strenuously enforced the Lambeth Articles. Within six months of their promulgation, for example, the Lady Margaret Professor of Divinity at Cambridge, Peter Baro, successfully circumvented them. Baro's soteriology anticipated Arminianism. Distinguishing between God's antecedent will, by which God offered salvation to all men, and God's consequent will, by which men either accepted or rejected this offer, Baro argued that "men shut themselve out of heaven not God." Officials justifiably charged Baro with contravening the Lambeth Articles. Baro, however, secured the support of Archbishop Whitgift and the Chancellor, Cecil, with the result that the case was dropped. According to Professor Curtis, the failure to enforce the Lambeth Articles in this case meant defeat for university Puritans. "The significance of the Baro incident," he argues,

> though perhaps few realized it at the time, was that it marked a turn in the tide of religious thought within the universities. Where formerly Calvinism, championed most ardently by the university Puritans, carried all before it, now a movement critical of Calvinism and especially of the extreme predestinarian principles of Calvin's latterday followers had not only won a hearing in the universities but had, against the temporary alliance of the university Puritans and the archbishop, so established its right to be heard

that it could not thereafter be suppressed. 15

Professor Porter's argument parallels precisely that of Professor Curtis. "The importance of the Barrett affair is this," he concludes,

> that the extreme Cambridge Calvinists had attempted to impose their interpretation of the mysteries of grace and assurance as the official and sole theology of the Church of England. So far as Cambridge was concerned they had failed. 16

For both Curtis and Porter, then, predestination and, by their definition, Puritanism, was a dormant entity at the universities by 1600. The university contribution to the events surrounding the English Revolution, from the perspective of such a subversive ideology as perceived by Hobbes, was perforce nonexistant.

I believe this interpretation to be fallacious. The primary faults of the arguments advocated by Professors Curtis and Porter result from their attitude toward predestination. To argue that the university soteriology was predestinarian before 1595 and Arminian after is to argue erroneously. As I have argued in the second chapter, university theologians effected, in essence, a soteriological compromise between faith and works. Their dual emphasis on works as well as on faith characterized their thought before 1595 as well as subsequent to that date. If by Puritanism one means an exclusively faith oriented and predestinarian soteriology, then 'Puritanism' never existed within the universities. The fallacy here, as Professor New points out, lays in equating Puritanism with predestination.

As I have demonstrated in the third chapter, Puritanism is more suitablly defined with reference to ecclesiology than soteriology. It is by their adherence to the <u>notae</u> of the true church that theologians are most correctly identified as Puritans. From the perspective of this definition, Puritanism existed within the universities throughout the entire period. Moreover, it is the ecclesiological threat posed by university Puritans, rather than their soteriology, which struck established authority as dangerous. This is hardly surprising given the basic agreement between Anglicans and Puritans on soteriological issues. The structure of the church, however, was another matter. Had the Puritan ecclesiology been imposed, drastic alterations in the established church would have resulted. Those changes would have divested the Crown of much of its religious authority. For one thing, ecclesiastcal discipline would have been much more vigorously enforced and enforced not by ecclesiastical courts controlled by the Crown, but by classes comprised of clergy. For another thing, the demand for a learned ministry presupposed that the universities, which were after all the suppliers of a learned ministry, would have exercised preponderant control over clerical appointments. They also would have controlled the doctrinal substance of the church's theology. Such doctrinal control followed from the university epistemology as well as from Puritan ecclesiology. As noted in my first chapter, the universities saw themselves as uniquely endowed with the attributes necessary to the pursuit of theological truth.

Puritanism, defined in terms of ecclesiology rather than soteriology, did exist at the universities throughout the period. The real significance of the Barrett and Baro cases so heavily emphasized by Professors Porter and Curtis is that they constitute the only cases throughout the period when established authroity vigorously concerned itself with soteriologcal issues. The majority of cases in which established authority intervened were ecclesiological and/or political in nature. Religious conformity, from the Crown's perspective, meant preeminently conformity to the Anglican ecclesiology and/or political theory.

I have suggested that Puritanism may also be defined with reference to political theory. While only some university Puritans developed a theory of legitimate resistance to established authroity, almost all university theologians endorsed concepts of covenant theology which served as the foundations for a more radical political theory. Moreover, Puritan ecclesiology and political theory often interfaced in terms of revolutionary ideology. For many Puritans, such as Nathaniel Bernard, the Crown's repudiation of Calvinist ecclesiology constituted a violation of the covenants and thus rendered resistance to established authority legitimate. Such views, while not popular among most university theologians during the period, laid the groundwork for radical political thought during the revolutionary period.

Reading Hobbes, one receives the impression that he thought the universities maliciously and intentionally developed religious and political theories to challenge established authority in church and state. On this point Hobbes misconstrued the situation. University theologians and their students did not engage in such deliberate subterfuge.

Their essential concern, in the final analysis, focused on soteriology. Their epistemology presupposed a soteriological emphasis. What constitutes a proper knowledge of God? How does such knowledge dictate our behavior with reference to our salvation? Concerns over ecclesiology and political theory originated out of attempts to answer these questions. That the universities ended by postulating a radical and subversive ideology, potentially, was, I think, an ironic and unintended by-product. Their essential inquiry remained the question of what must a man do in this sinful world to be saved. In the question as well as the answer the university theologians were neither Anglican nor Puritan. They were merely Christian.

NOTES

¹ Excerpts of the law are given in George Adams and H. Stephens, eds., *Select Documents Of English Constitutional History* (New York: The MacMillan Co., 1921), pp. 121 and 122.

² John Rushworth, *The Tryal Of Thomas Earl Of Strafford* (London: John Rushworth, 1680), p. 8.

³ The English common law heritage, of course, contributed to this new definition of treason based on fundamental law as well. See, e.g., J. W. Gough, *Fundamental Law In English Constitutional History* (Oxford: The Clarendon Press, 1955) and J. G. A. Pocock, *The Ancient Constitution And The Feudal Law: A Study Of English Historical Thought In The Seventeenth Century* (Cambridge: University Press, 1957). One need not posit an either/or scenario for the development of fundamental law and its application to the concept of teason. Both covenant thology and the Common law, I believe, contributed to that development.

⁴ Cobbett, comp., *State Trials,* 33 vols. (London: R. Bagshaw, 1809), 3:1416.

⁵ Rushworth, *Tryal Of Strafford,* p. 658.

⁶ Paul Christianson, *Reformers and Babylon: English apocalyptic visions from the Reformation to the eve of the Civil War* (Toronto: University of Toronto Press, 1978), p. 130.

⁷ Ibid., pp. 207 and 208.

⁸ Thomas Hobbes, *Behemoth: Or The Long Parliament* (London: 1689), p. 23.

⁹ Ibid., p. 40.

¹⁰ Ibid., p. 58

¹¹ John F. Wilson, *Pulpit In Parliament: Puritanism During The English Civil Wars 1640-1648* (Princeton: Princeton University Press, 1969). See especially chap. 6, "Puritan Piety for a Covenanted Nation." Among the more prominent divines discussed by Wilson are John Marshall, who attended Emmanuel College at Cambridge, Obadiah Sedgwick, who graduated A.B. from Magdalen Hall at Oxford, and

Edmund Calamy, who received his A.B. from Pembroke College at Cambridge.

[12] London, British Library, Sloane MSS, 227, p. 7.

[13] William Perkins, _A Golden Chaine: Or , The Description Of Theologie Containing The Order Of The Causes Of Salvation And Damnation According To God's Word,_ printed in _The Works,_ p. 26.

[14] Mark H. Curtis, _Oxford And Cambridge In Transition: 1558-1642_ (Oxford: Clarendon Press, 1959), p. 189. Of especiall interest are chapters seven, "The Universities And English Religion" and eight, "The Universities And The Religious Movements Of The Age."

[15] Ibid., p. 222. For relevant documentation concerning the Barrett and Baro cases see, e.g., Cambridge, Cambridge University Archives, Guard Book 6.1, "Ecclesiastical causes and censures," items 28, 31, 32, and 33.

[16] Porter, _Reformation And Reaction In Tudor Cambridge,_ p. 363.

BIBLIOGRAPHY

Primary Sources: Unpublished

Cambridge. University Library. MS.Mm.1.38.
"Copies of letters and c. that past during Dr. Jegon's vice- chancellorship ann. 1600, 1601."

Cambridge. University Library. MS.Mm.1.40.
"Copies of letters (most originall) from Lord Burghley, R. earle of Leycester, Sir W. Ralegh, Archbps. Parker, Whitgift, Bancroft, lord North, Sir Edw. Coke, Rob. earl of Salisbury, H. earle of Northampton, & c. taken from a volume of letters in the registrary's office, so mixt and confus'd, that they cannot be reduc't to any tolerable order."

Cambridge. University Library. MS.Mm.6.54.
"The Sermon on 1. Samuel, 4:22, preached at St. Mary's Cambridge 6 May 1632 by Nath. Bernard."

Cambridge. University Library. MS.Mm.1.37.
"Orationes et scripta quaedam Joannis Overall."

Cambridge. University Library. MS.Mm.6.41.
"Notes of Sermons Preached At Oxford."

Cambridge. University Library. MS.Mm.2.23.
"Trials before the Vicechancellor."

Cambridge. University Library. MS.Mm.1.35.
"The copies of diverse Letters from privie Counsaillours & Men of Ho: sent to the Vicechan: & Heads of Coll: there, in the tyme of Dr. Jegon 1596, 1597, & c."

Cambridge. University Library. MS.Gg.1.29.
"A Collection of Miscellaneous Theological and Historical Documents."

Cambridge. University Library. MS.Ff.5.25.
"A Sermon preached to his Maiestye at Roiston by Mr. Simpson, Fellow of Trinitye College in Cambridge, 1617."

Cambridge. University Archives. Guard Book 6.1.
"Ecclesiastical causes and censures."

Cambridge. University Archives. Guard Book C.U.R. 4 Item 2. "Complaint against T. Smyth--Christs

F.--for attacking in a Common Place the surplice, cross, churching of women, etc. 1597."

Oxford. Bodleian Library. MS.Top Oxon.f.52.
"Two sermons of which the first was preached at Oxford 1619-1620 or 1624-25 probably by Thomas Anyan President of Corpus Christi Coll."

Oxford. Bodleian Library. MS.Top. Oxon.f.53.
"Oxford sermons probably written out by an Oxford divinity student c. 1596."

Oxford. Bodleian Library. MS.Eng.th.f.7.
"Sermon Noates (1634-1637), taken from the Preaching of Hoffman, Sutton, Chidloo, Pell, Digle, Stanly, Archer, Fisher and other eminent Oxford Preachers."

Oxford. Bodleian Library. MS.ADD.B.82.
"Mr. Lushington's sermon preached at St. Maries Oxon: April 18 1625."

Oxford. Bodleian Library. MS.ADD.A.115.
"Autograph Manuscript A.D. 1595: The Commonn-Place Book of the Rev. Lionel Day, Fellow of Balliol College, Oxford.

Oxford. Bodleian Library. MS.Eng.th.3.14.
"Sermons preached by severall men upon severall occasions in St. Maryes & other places in Oxford, 1630, 1633."

Oxford. Bodleian Library. MS.Rawlinson.E.154.
"Sermons in English, with a few in Latin, preached at Oxford in 1606-07 by Dr. Richard Makek."

Oxford. Bodleian Library. MS.Rawlinson.E.168.
"Sermons by Thomas Lydist of New College Oxford."

Oxford. Bodleian Library. MS.Rawlinson.E.224.
"Sermons and theological notes by a member of St. John's College, Cambr."

London. British Library. Lansdowne MSS.
"Lord Burghley's Papers."

London. British Library. Sloane MSS.227.
"Theological lectures and sermons delivered by a member of St. Mary Hall before the University of Oxford about the year 1600."

London. British Library. ADD.MSS.30,498.
"Notes of divinity lectures by John Rainolds DD, afterwards Dean of Lincoln and President of Corpus Christi College, Oxford, delivered at Oxford 1587-1592."

London. British Library. Harleian MSS.Num.7031.
"Letters & other particulars concerning Kings College, Trinity Col., Christs Col., Corpus Christi, Trinity Hall, Peterhouse, Pembroke, Queens, Sydney, Magdalen, Cauis."

London. British Library. Harleian MSS.Num.7047.
"Particulars relating to Clare Hall."

Primary Sources: Published

Bancroft, Richard. *Daungerous Positions And Proceedings, published and practised within this Iland of Brytaine, under pretence of Reformation and for the Presbiteriall Discipline.* London: John Wolfe, 1593.

——————————. *A Survey Of The Pretended Holy Discipline.* London: John Wolfe, 1593.

Beza, Theodore. *A Discourse Of the true visible Markes of the Catholique Churche.* London: Robert Walda-grave, 1582.

Brightman, Thomas. *A Revelation Of The Revelation That Is The Revelation Of St. John Opened With A Logicall Re-solution And Exposition.* Amsterdam: 1615.

Calvin, John. *The Institutes Of The Christian Religion.* 2 vols. Philadelphia: The Westminster Press. 1960.

Cartwright, Thomas. "A Directory Of Church Government" in *Neal's History Of The Puritans.* vol. 5. London: R. Cruttwell, 1797.

Chaderton, Laurence. *An Excellent And Godly Sermon Most Needefull For This Time Wherein We Live In All Securitie And Sinne To The Great Dishonour Of God And Contempt Of His Holy Word.* London: Christopher Barker, 1578.

_____. *A Fruitfull Sermon upon the 3.4.5.6.7. and 8. verses of the 12. Chapter of the Epistle of S. Paul to the Romanes.* London: Robert Walde-grave, 1584.

Crawshawe, William. *The Sermon Preached At the Crosse Feb. xiiij. 1607.* London: Edmond Weaver, 1608.

Douglas, C. E. and Frere, W. H. eds. *Puritan Manifestoes.* London: 1907.

Franklin, Julian H. ed. *Constitutionalism And Resistance In The Sixteenth Century: Three Treatises By Hotman, Beza, & Mornay.* New York: Western Publishing Co., 1969.

Hobbes, Thomas. *Behemoth: Or The Long Parliament.* London: 1689.

Knox, John and Whittingham, William. "The forme of prayers and Ministration of the Sacraments, &c. used in the Englishe Congregation at Geneva and approved by that famous and godly learned man, John Calvyn." In *The Works Of John Knox.* David Laing, ed. vol. 4. Edinburgh: 1855.

Perkins, William. *An Exposition Of the Symbole Or Creede of the Apostles, according to the tenour of the Scripture, and the consent of Orthodoxe Fathers of the Church.* In *The Works Of That Famous And Worthie Minister Of Christ, in the University of Cambridge, M.W. Perkins.* Cambridge: John Legat, 1603.

_____. *A Golden Chaine: Or, The Description Of Theologie Containing The Order Of The Causes Of Salvation And Damnation According To God's Word.* In *The Works.*

_____. *A Treatise Of God's Free Grace And Man's Free Will.* In *The Works.*

_____. *Of The Calling Of The Ministerie Two Treatises: Describing The Duties And Dignities of that calling: Delivered Publikely in the Universities of Cambridge by Maister Perkins.* London: Thomas

Creede, 1606.

Reynolds, John. *The Summe Of The Conference Betweene John Rainoldes And John Hart: Touching The Head And The Faith Of The Church: Whereto Is Annexed A Treatise Intitled, Six Conclusions Touching The Holie Scripture And The Church.* London: George Bishop, 1584.

_____. *The Prophecie Of Obadiah Opened And Applyed In Sundry Learned And Gracious Sermons Preached At All-Hallowes And St. Maries in Oxford.* Oxford: Joseph Barnes, 1613.

_____. *A Sermon Upon Part Of The Eighteenth Psalme Preached To the Publike Assembly Of Scholers In The University of Oxford The Last Day Of August 1586.* Oxford: Joseph Barnes, 1613.

Robinson, Hastings. ed. *Zurich Letters.* Cambridge: University Press, 1845.

Rushworth, John. *The Tryal Of Thomas Earl Of Strafford.* London: John Rushworth, 1680.

Some, Robert. *A Godly Treatise containing and deciding certaine questions, mooved of late in London and other places touching the Ministerie, Sacraments, and Church.* London: Christopher Barker, 1588.

Usher, R.G. ed. *The Presbyterian Movement In The Reign Of Queen Elizabeth As Illustrated By The Minute Book Of The Dedham Classis: 1582-1589.* London: The Royal Historical Society, 1905.

Whitaker, William. *An Answere To The Ten Reasons Of Edmund Campion The Jusuit.* London: 1606.

Whittingham, William. "A Brieff Discours off the troubles begonne at Franckford in Germany Anno Domini 1554." In *The Works Of John Knox.*

Secondary Sources

Avis, Paul. *The Church In The Theology Of The Reformers.* Atlanta: John Knox Press, 1981.

Audi, Robert and Wainwright, William, eds. *Rationality, Religious Belief, & Moral Commitment: New Essays in the Philosophy of Religion.* Ithaca: Cornell University Press, 1986.

Backus, Irene. "Laurence Tomsen (1539-1608) and Elizabethan Puritanism." *Journal Of Ecclesiastical History* 28 (1977).

Baker, J. Wayne. *Heinrich Bullinger and the Covenant: The Other Reformed Tradition.* Athens, Ohio: Ohio University Press, 1980.

Ball, Bryan. *A Great Expectation: Eschatological Thought In English Protestantism to 1660.* Leiden: 1975.

Bauckham, Richard. "Marian Exiles and Cambridge James Pilkington's 'Halfe a Score.'" *Journal Of Ecclesiastical History* 26 (1975).

Bornkamm, Heinrich. "Faith and Reason in the Erasmus and Luther." *Religion and Culture: Essays In Honor of Paul Tillich.* Walter Leibrecht, ed. New York: Harper & Brothers, 1959.

Campbell, William. *The Triumph of Presbyterianism.* Edinburgh: The Saint Andrew Press, 1958.

Cecil de Pauley, William. *The Candle Of The Lord: Studies in the Cambridge Platonists.* London: The Society for Promoting Christian Knowledge, 1937.

Christianson, Paul. *Reformers and Babylon: English apocalyptic visions from the reformation to the eve of the Civil War.* Toronto: University of Toronto Press, 1978.

Clebsch, William. *England's Earliest Protestants: 1520-1535.* New Haven: Yale University Press, 1964.

Colie, Rosalie. *Light And Enlightenment: A Study Of The Cambridge Platonists And The Dutch Arminians.* Cambridge: University Press, 1957.

Collinson, Patrick. *The Elizabethan Puritan Movement.* Los Angeles: University of California Press, 1967.

Coolidge, John. *The Pauline Renaissance In England: Puritanism And The Bible.* Oxford: Clarendon Press, 1970.

Costello, William. *The Scholastic Curriculum At Early Seventeenth Century Cambridge.* Cambridge: Harvard University Press, 1958.

Cremeans, Charles David. *The Reception Of Calvinistic Thought In England.* Urbana, Illinois: University of Illinois Press, 1949.

Curtis, Mark. "The Alienated Intellectuals Of Early Stuart England." *Past And Present* 23 (1962).

──────────. *Oxford And Cambridge In Transition: 1558-1642.* Oxford: Clarendon Press, 1959.

Dillenberger, John. *God Hidden And Revealed: The interpretation of Luther's deus absconditus and its significance for religious thought.* Philadelphia: Muhlenberg Press, 1953.

Dowey, Edward. *The Knowledge Of God In Calvin's Theology.* New York: Columbia University Press, 1952.

Ebeling, Gerhard. *Luther: An Introduction To His Thought.* Philadelphia: Fortress Press, 1964.

Edwards, Mark. *Luther and the False Brethren.* Stanford: Stanford University Press, 1977.

Emerson, Everett. "Calvin and Covenant Theology." *Church History* 25 (1956).

Forstman, Jackson. *Word and Spirit: Calvin's Doctrine of Biblical Authority.* Stanford:

Stanford University Press, 1962.

Gerrish, Brian. _Grace And Reason: A Study in The Theology of Luther._ New York: Oxford University Press, 1962.

Giesey, Ralph. "The Monarchomach Triumvirs: Hotman, Beza, and Mornay." _Bibliotheque D'Humanisme Et Renaissance: Travaux Et Documents_ 32 (1970).

Gough, J. W. _Fundamental Law In English Constitutional History._ Oxford: Clarendon Press, 1955.

Greaves, Richard. "John Bunyan And Covenant Thought In The Seventeenth Century." _Church History_ 36 (1967).

_____. "John Knox and the Covenant Tradition." _Journal of Ecclesiastical History_ 24 (1973).

_____. "The Origins and Early Development of English Covenant Thought." _The Historian_ 31 (1968).

Haller, William. _The Elect Nation: The Meaning and Relevance of Foxe's Book of Martyrs._ New York: Harper & Row, 1963.

_____. _The Rise of Puritanism._ New York: Columbia University Press, 1938.

Haugaard, William. _Elizabeth And The English Reformation: The Struggle For A Stable Settlement Of Religion._ Cambridge: University Press, 1968.

Headley, John. _Luther's View Of Church History._ New Haven: Yale University Press, 1963.

Hill, Christopher, _The World Turned Upside Down: Radical Ideas during the English Revolution._ New York: Viking Press, 1972.

Howell, William. _Logic and Rhetoric in England: 1500-1700._ Princeton: Princeton University Press, 1975.

Kendall, R.T. _Calvin And English Calvinism To_

1649. Oxford: Oxford University Press, 1979.

Kittelson, James. *Wolfgang Capito: From Humanist To Reformer.* Leiden: Brill, 1975.

_____. "Marbach vs. Zanchi: The Resolution of Controversy in late Reformation Strassbourg." *Sixteenth Century Journal.* 8 (1977).

Knappen, M. M. *Tudor Puritanism: A Chapter In The History Of Idealism.* Chicago: University of Chicago Press, 1925.

Lake, Peter. "The Dilemma of the Establishment Puritan: the Cambridge Heads and the case of Francis Johnson and Cuthbert Bainbrigg." *Journal of Ecclesiastical History.* 29 (1978).

_____. *Moderate Puritans And The Elizabethan Church.* Cambridge: Cambridge University Press, 1982.

Mallet, Charles. *A History Of The University Of Oxford.* New York: Barnes & Noble, Inc., 1924.

Manning, Roger. *Religion And Society In Elizabethan Sussex: A Study Of The Enforcement Of The Religious Settlement, 1558-1603.* Bristol: Leicester University Press, 1969.

Maruyama, Tadataka. "The Reform Of The True Church: The Ecclesiology of Theodore Beza." Th.D. diss. Princeton Theological Seminary, 1973.

McCoy, Charles. "Johannes Cocceius: Federal Theologian." *Scottish Journal Of Theology* 16 (1963).

McDonnell, Kilian. *John Calvin, the Church and the Eucharist.* Princeton: Princeton University Press, 1967.

McGinn, Donald. *The Admonition Controversy.* New Brunswick: Rutgers University Press, 1949.

NcNeill, John. "The Church In Sixteenth-century Reformed Theology." *Journal of Religion* 22 (1942).

Moller, Jens. "The Beginnings of Puritan Covenant Theology." *Journal Of Ecclesiastical History* 14 (1963).

Morgan, Edmund. *Visible Saints: The History of a Puritan Idea.* Ithaca: Cornell University Press, 1963.

Mosse, George. *The Holy Pretence: A Study in Christianity and Reason of State from William Perkins to John Winthrop.* Oxford: Basil Blackwell, 1957.

Mullinger, J. *A History Of The University Of Cambridge.* London: Longmans, Green, And Co., 1888.

New John. *Anglican and Puritan: The Basis of their Opposition, 1558-1640.* Stanford: Stanford University Press, 1964.

Nuttall, Geoffrey. *The Holy Spirit in Puritan Faith and Experience.* Oxford: Oxford University Press, 1946.

Parker, T.H. *Calvin's Doctrine Of The Knowledge Of God.* Grand Rapids, Mich.: Wm. B. Eerdmans Publishing Co., 1952.

Pearson, A.F. Scott. *Thomas Cartwright And Elizabethan Puritanism.* Cambridge: Cambridge University Press, 1925.

Petry, Ray. "Calvin's Conception Of The "Communis Sanctorum." *Church History* 5 (1936).

Pettit, Norman. *The Heart Prepared: Grace and Conversion in Puritan Spiritual Life.* New Haven: Yale University Press, 1966.

Porter, H. C. *Reformation And Reaction In Tudor Cambridge.* Cambridge: Cambridge University Press, 1958.

Primus, John. *The Vestments Controversy: An Historical Study Of The Earliest Tensions Within The Church Of England In The Reigns Of Edward VI And Elizabeth.* Kampen: J.H. Kok, 1960.

Pocock, J. G. A. *The Ancient Constitution And The Feudal Law: A Study Of English Historical Thought In The Seventeenth Century.* Cambridge: Cambridge: Cambridge University Press, 1957.

Reilly, Bart. *The Elizabethan Puritan's Conception of the Nature and Destiny of Fallen Man.* Washington: The Catholic University of American Press, 1948.

Rohr, John Von. "Covenant And Assurance In Early English Puritanism." *Church History* 34 (1965).

Rupp, Gordon. *The Righteousness Of God.* London: Hodder & Stoughton, 1953.

Seaver, Paul. *The Puritan Lectureships: The Politics of Religious Disent 1560-1662.* Stanford: Stanford University Press, 1970.

Seigel Jerrold. *Rhetoric and Philosophy In Renaissance Humanism: The Union Of Eloquence And Wisdom, Petrarch To Valla.* Princeton: Princeton University Press, 1968.

Sommerville, C. J. "Conversion versus the Early Puritan Covenant of Grace." *Journal Of Presbyterian History* 44 (1965).

Trinkaus, Charles. *In Our Image and Likeness: Humanity and Divinity in Italian Humanist Thought.* 2 vols. London: Constable & Co, 1970.

Walzer, Michael. *The Revolution of the Saints: A Study in the Origins of Radical Politics.* Cambridge: Harvard University Press, 1965.

Wendel, Francois. *Calvin: Sources et Evolution de sa Pensee Religieuse.* Paris: Universitaires de France, 1950.

White, B. R. *The English Separatist Tradition: From The Marian Martyrs to the Pilgrim Fathers.* Oxford: Oxford University Press, 1971.

Wilson, John. *Pulpit In Parliament: Puritanism*

during the English Civil Wars 1640-1648. Princeton: Princeton University Press, 1969.

Van Zandt, A. B. "The Doctrine of the Covenants Considered as the central principle of Theology." *Presbyterian Review* 3 (1892).

Index

Ascham, Roger, 1
Baker, 36
Balliol College, Oxford, 6, 29
Barbar, Thomas, 57
Baro, Peter, 102, 104
Barrett, Edmund, 55
Bernard, Nathaniel, 65, 90, 91, 92, 97, 99, 100, 104
Beza, T., 87, 89
Brasenose College, Oxford, 36
Brightman, Thomas, 63, 64, 65
Browne, 56, 57
Brownrig, 86, 87, 90, 98
Bunyan, John, 12, 40
Burghley, 55, 82, 86
Caius College, Cambridge, 39
Calvin, Calvinism, 6, 87
Cartwright, Thomas, 50, 56, 57, 61
Cecil, Robert, 80, 81, 102
Chaderton, Lawrence, 14, 63, 64, 65, 86
Chidloo, 18, 19
Christ Church, Oxford, 20, 31
Christs' College, Cambridge, 52, 61
Cole, William, 49
Copcot, John, 81
Corpus Christi College, Oxford, 62, 68
Crashawe, Willias, 67
deus absconditus, 17, 18
deus revelatus, 17, 18, 19
Durden, Ralph, 80, 92
Edwards, 87
Emnanuel College Cambridge, 14, 68, 90
Estye, George, 39
Field, John, 56
Garland, 30
Gellibrand, Edward, 56, 57, 59
Goade, Roger, 55
Harrison, Thomas, 57
Hobbes, T., 99, 101, 105
Holmes, N., 98
Jegon, John, 55, 82, 83
Knox, John, 53
Lutter, Martin, 6
Lushington, 4
Magdalen College Oxford, 56
ordo salutis, 23, 24, 32, 33, 35, 36, 37, 38, 39
Overall, John, 35, 36, 37
Owen, 86
Paraeus, David, 84
Pembroke Hall, Cambridge, 80

Perkins, William, 5, 6, 36, 38, 57, 58, 67, 100
Peterhouse Colege Cambridge, 2
Preston, Thones, 55
Reynolds, John, 62, 66, 68
Rudd, 81, 82
Shinley, 20, 22, 31, 32, 40
Silby, 8
Simpson, 34, 38
Some, Roger, 5
Stockton, 55
St. Mary's Church Oxford, 62
St. Mary's Church Cambridge, 82
Stanly, 18
Still, John, 55
Strafford, 97
Sutton, 29
Trinity College Cambridge, 21, 34, 35, 57
Tucker, 23
University College Oxford, 23
West, 56
Witters, George, 53
Whitgift, 83, 102
Whitingham, 53
Whitaker, William, 21, 39
Woodhead, 23
Yaine, 34